For my beautiful girl, Amber Fassett

If I never did anything else right,
I taught you all about Jesus. I love you!

TABLE OF CONTENTS

Devotion/Study	Page

INTRODUCTION

It has always been my desire to share the word in such a way it makes people think. To think outside of the box, to see the word as it applies to one's life, to see the word opened up and understood. *Think On This* is how God deals with me about topics and subjects common to each of us.

I started this project several years ago, intending to create a 365-day devotional. God had a different plan however, and you know his ideas are always better.

My prayer is during the course of the year you will grow as you work your way through the study. I pray it makes you stop and think. I pray it forces you to ask yourself important questions. To question what you believe at times, how you believe, how you live, to judge your own moral compass and in the end to see new growth, new fruit on your spiritual tree.

Please take your time, don't simply rush through. If you can, answer one question a day. I know it's not always possible. At the very least, allow yourself to ponder on the lesson during the week. Think about what it says and how it applies. Try applying it. We only grow when we apply what we learn. If you disagree with a lesson, study it out a little further. See what the bible has to say about it.

I would love to hear from you. Message me on Facebook at Think On This. Be sure to LIKE my page. Share what you learned from a particular lesson. Share how you are growing or how the lesson impacted you. See what other people are saying and thinking.

From the bottom of my heart, thank you for choosing Think On This! 2 Timothy 3:16-17

ABOUT THE AUTHOR

Amy Nichols is a multi-talented woman of God. Since 2012 she has traveled full-time with her husband Randy as Appointed2. Together they are a high energy Christian Country evangelistic duo.

Amy is a singer, songwriter, speaker, author, blogger, vlogger and artist. Approximately three years ago Amy began creating her own greeting card line, Speak Life Inspirational Greetings by Amy. All of the cards are done by hand, containing a word that speaks life and encouragement into the receiver.

Every Tuesday morning at 10am eastern Randy and Amy can be found on Facebook at Appointed2 where they present AppointiNEWS. They share a song, a devotion, offer prayer and tell all the latest news concerning Appointed2. As Appointed2, Randy and Amy also help host Fire Fest Campmeeting for the Soul in Crystal River, FL. Check it out at Firefestcampmeeting.com

At Appointed2.com you can find Amy's blog. It isn't updated as frequently as she would like but on occasion, she adds new material.

In 2020, Amy is working on a few other new projects. If everything works as planned announcements will be made on her Facebook pages and website. Amy would simply tell you that all things are possible when you trust God, when you look to him and above all when you pray and ask believing.

ACKNOWLEDGMENTS

No one ever accomplishes any great feat without people encouraging them along the way. I have some of the greatest people surrounding me. This book would never have come to fruition without Jesus. I am thankful every day for the life he has entrusted me with and for the grace that allowed me time to come to the full knowledge of his love.

My greatest fan has always been my mom. As a teenager I was in many special band and choir events. My mom was always in the audience. She traveled in all types of weather for miles and hours just to see me up on those stages. My mom has loved me at times when I wasn't very lovable, she has loved me through the darkest moments and rejoiced with me in the greatest. I love you mom.

God has blessed me over and over again. One of the greatest blessings is my husband, Randy. He has taught me not to wait but to get up and move when God gives you a task. He has loved me beyond measure and made me feel treasured. Our journey is the kind many dream of and few live.

I have learned a great deal by being a mom. Amber has cheered me on, believed with me and been a voice of wisdom. We have cried, laughed, prayed and rejoiced together. There is nothing like a daughter.

One last mention, Toni Walker. Every time I speak to her, she speaks encouragement to me. She sees me in ways that I wonder who she is looking at. (Now I'm laughing.) She tells me I'm amazing, or I'm talented or a dozen other phrases and she means every one of them. Thank you, woman of God for being my friend. Thank you all!

WITHHOUT THIS

2 TIMOTHY 3:16-17

"All scripture is given by inspiration of God, and is profitable for doctrine, for reproof, for correction, for instruction in righteousness: That the man of God may be perfect, thoroughly furnished unto all good works."

2 Timothy is probably the last letter Paul ever wrote. He was cast into a prison where his only link to the outside world was an 18" square hole in the ceiling; where letters were passed in and out. With his final words he continues to impress the importance of God's word.

THINK ON THIS...

I love it when I begin to pray, and words bubble up out of me, words I didn't know I was going to say or where I was headed with them. Those thoughts turn out to be some of the best prayers. They're deep thoughts, like the one I am sharing with you today. As I held onto my bible preparing to read, I began to pray. These are the words I uttered, "Without this word....."

Without this word, how would I know how much you love me? God shows us how deep his love is for us in every word penned. He shows us when dealing with our enemies. He shows us through promises, he shows us through every step Jesus took to make a way for us. Think about what the word says.

Without this word, how would I know what God's promises are? Because of the word I know I am a descendant of Abraham. I know by his stripes I am healed. I know he will supply all my needs according to his riches in glory. I know he sees me coming in, going out, lying down and rising up. I know the Holy Ghost is a promise to me and to my children's children as far off as believe. How many more promises can you think of today?

Without this word, how would I know what is expected of me? How would I know I need to repent or be baptized? How would I know that the fatherless and widows are my responsibility? How would I know it's my job to share this good news? How would I know my role as a wife, mother, teacher, friend and so on? I know the sinner fills these same roles, but in society today it's easy to see the issues which occur because people are unfamiliar with what the word says?

Without this word, how would I know what awaits me on the other side? Because of the word I know there is a robe and crown for me. Perhaps more than one crown. I know he has prepared a place for me. I know there is a Crystal Sea and a street of gold. I know there is a thrown and 24 elders around it. I know it's beautiful there, there is no sorrow, no dying, no pain. I know I want to go there.

Without this word, how would I know what Hell is like? How would we know, we definitely DO NOT want to go there without this word? Hell is hot, it was only meant for the devil and the angels who left Heaven with him. It was not meant for you and me, but people have chosen to go there. Chosen to go where there is endless torment. Where there is gnashing of teeth, pain, anguish, hopelessness, sorrow, remorse, guilt, there is no good thing in Hell. There are no parties going on there. There are no buddies, no hanging out, no good times happening there.

Without this word, how would I know who God is? He is omniscient, omnipresent, omnipotent, everlasting, Spirit, holy, Alpha and Omega, lord of lords, king of kings, creator of all life, judge, physician, lawyer, father, provider. He is everything.

Without this word, how could I know and be inspired by people like David, Nehemiah, Esther, Paul, Isaiah, Abraham, Moses, Noah, Abigail, Stephen, Peter, John, Mary, Joseph and every other person mentioned. Whether the individuals did good or they did evil we can learn from them.

I count it an honor and a pleasure to hold this word in my hands. I get to have it in its entirety. Some people only have a page or a piece of a page and long for the whole word. I love the word and thank God for having men write it down that I could read it, study it and know it.

QUESTIONS

1. How do you see the word of God? Is it a treasure or just another book?

2. Do you know what's contained within the cover of your bible? Have you explored it for yourself? Don't just hear about it, go look for yourself! What have you found inside?

3. If you didn't have a bible handy would you be able to share the word? Is it hidden in your heart? You may not know chapter and verse, but do you know what the word says?

4. Do you have a favorite scripture you can quote? Write it down.

5. Write down something that "Without this word" you wouldn't have known or understood. What or how did it change you?

FRIENDS

GENESIS 1:27

"So God created man in his own image, in the image of God created he him; male and female created he them."
God took care of the void, separated the waters and made dry ground. He created every tree, every creature in the water and on the ground, every bird, every berry and seed before he created man. Even in the beginning God supplied every need Adam had before Adam could ask him for anything.

THINK ON THIS...

Imagine God sitting in heaven. There are angels of every rank and file surrounding him. The sights and sounds of heaven are beyond compare and yet, God desires something more.

God desired a friend. He looked down at the earth, once perfect in shape and form but it is now void and dark. It was the place where Lucifer and his minions landed when they were forcibly removed from heaven. Their presence changed everything. God has a plan though and he goes to work.

It's funny how things just dawn on you. It's like a light bulb goes on in your head, and suddenly something you have always known really sinks in; you see it in a whole different light. God created us to have fellowship with him. Notice in James 2:23 it says,
"...Abraham believed God and it was imputed unto him for righteousness: and he was called the Friend of God."

God had Adam name all the animals; to see if any of them would make a good friend. When none was found he created woman. It was the same for God. All the celestial beings in heaven and none were found for fellowship. So, he created man. Those under your authority can't be your friend. Acquaintance yes, but friend no. Otherwise you will show partiality and be biased. Discipline and giving directions would be difficult; no matter how good your friendship is.

Everything a man does for his wife should be done the same way Christ does it for the church. Do you see the parallel? Just as we desire the love of one person who is fully devoted to us, God desires the church to be fully devoted and in love with him. He doesn't want us to love him, or to placate him, because he gives us gifts. You can't buy love with things. You find out who truly loves you when you have nothing to give but your own love, your own self.

You weren't created for God to control. You weren't created for what you could do for God or what you could give him. After all, what could you ever do or give that he doesn't already have? Not to mention, he has all those angels at his beck and call. He is the commander of the celestial troops. He has his own army. Angels who are warriors, angels who praise his name, angels who are messengers, angels who serve, he has angels everywhere!

Today, I just want you to remember, you were created just because God desired to have fellowship with you. He desired to have a conversation over a cup of coffee or a coke. He loves it when you sing to him, when you talk with him, invite him along for a drive or whatever you are doing. He just wants to be with you.

I love the fact, that my husband just likes having me near. I don't have to be doing anything. We don't even have to be talking. It is just my presence in the room with him. Of course, that goes both ways. Being separated for even a day or two creates a void. We may talk on the phone or video chat, but it isn't the same as being present.

Give God permission to be present with you in everything. Yes! You need to ask him to come. He doesn't intrude. He doesn't come where he hasn't been asked or invited. Just let his presence dwell wherever you are. Because the void creates loneliness and a feeling of being empty. Jesus would you please come and be with us today.

QUESTIONS

1. What are the most important qualities you look for in a friend?

2. Do you think those same qualities are important to God? Why?

3. Do you ever just say "Hello Jesus"? Do you ever ask how his day is or how people are treating him today? Ask him what you can do for him today?

4. Have you ever thought that God might like to talk about himself sometimes? We always talk about our needs, our wants but do we stop to think that God has things he would like from us?

5. What do you think God would like from you?

GRAY GRACE

EPHESIANS 2:5
*"For by grace are ye saved through faith; and that not
of yourselves: It is the gift of God:"*

Paul is writing to the Ephesians. It isn't enough to start a
church and appoint a pastor. You have to check on them,
encourage them and reiterate again and again how to stay
on the right track.

THINK ON THIS...
In today's society there is a misnomer concerning grace.
People have somehow misconstrued grace as being a
paintbrush or filter that overlays the black and white word of
God to create a gray space.

Grace is the love of God, which gives us something we didn't
earn or deserve. It is not a card we play, like in Monopoly,
that gets us out of Hell free and clear. It isn't a paintbrush
that whitewashes our sin so it becomes acceptable in the
eyes of God either. Paul said it this way in Romans 6:1-2,
*"Shall we continue to sin, that grace may abound? God
forbid."*

The word of God is truly black and white. It clearly names
the sins of this life and emphatically states they will keep a
soul from entering into heaven. Repentance causes our sins
to be forgiven and baptism washes those same sins away.
After that, we have an advocate with the father that IF we
should sin we can be forgiven. (1 John 2:1)

Hebrews 4:12 describes the power of God's word with such
descriptive imagery it is easy to imagine the thin line
between the black and the white of it.
"For the word of God is quick, and powerful, and

sharper than any two-edged sword, piercing even to the dividing asunder of soul and spirit, and of the joints and marrow, and is a discerner of the thoughts and intents of the heart."

Gray areas lend themselves to interpretation. Gray areas are places of uncertainty. Gray areas leave you feeling anxious and nervous. Gray areas are places without distinct borders and boundaries. None of these descriptions describe a true walk with God or with an understanding of his word. God is always clear and concise.

When a pastor stands up and tells his congregation he has nothing to preach today but instead confesses he is addicted to pornography; there ought to be a response. When a pastor gets up to stand in the pulpit wearing a T-shirt emblazoned with a beer logo; there ought to be a response. However, in both of these scenarios (and they are true scenarios), the congregation goes home and shows back up the following Sunday. When did either of these scenarios become acceptable? I don't know when. I only know they are leaning on grace and believing they fall into a gray area. They believe God loves them and he won't send them to hell when they meet at judgment.

Grace allows us time to become cognizant of our sins. To recognize and repent from them. Otherwise, judgement and the wages of our sin would be instantaneous, no one would make it into heaven.

Today, you are responsible for this word. Grace is not gray. It does NOT create a space where sin is acceptable. Grace is a gift, pure and simple. Treat it with care and respect.

QUESTIONS

1. Honestly survey your life right now. Are there any areas where sin lives? You know in your heart if you are committing sin. Write down those areas that are sin. If the bible calls it sin, write it down.

2. Has polite society created the idea those items you listed are ok? Do they call them acceptable? If you surveyed 100 people do you think they would call your actions sin?

3. Regardless of what society perceives and admonishes what do you think of the items you listed? Do you think they would keep you from entering heaven if you died tonight?

4. Remember there are no gray areas. If the word, the bible, declares something is sin, then it is sin. No one can change the classification of it. God's word is forever settled in heaven. Do you think it's possible to justify your actions with God?

5. If God lets you in with your sins, what will he say to those he condemned for those same sins? Like those from the flood of Noah's day or those in Sodom and Gomorrah, or to David whose child died? How will he answer them?

NO HELP NEEDED

GENESIS 16:5

*"And Sarai said unto Abram, My wrong be upon
thee: I have given my maid into thy bosom; and
when she saw that she had conceived, I was
despised in her eyes: the Lord judge between me
and thee."*

Sarai (Sarah) was getting older and she was barren. In
those days a woman's worth was found in her ability to bear
and raise children. God had promised Abram (Abraham) a
child, so Sarah came up with a plan to help God and get a
son. She gave her servant to her husband and her servant
became pregnant.

THINK ON THIS...

Have you ever tried to help God? Sarah did. God had made
a promise to Abraham and years went by but still no baby.
As a woman, we all have this awareness where our
biological clocks are tick tocking as we age. So did Sarah. I
would imagine she felt the pressure of needing to conceive,
all the while she hears tick tock tick tock tick tock. When we
start to feel the pressure, we start looking for alternative
ways and methods to achieve the expected end.

Sarah came up with a plan. All she needed was a surrogate
to carry her husband's child. Enter Hagar, Sarah's servant.
Sarah tells Abraham her idea and he just says "As you wish",
just like Wesley in The Princess Bride! So, Abraham marries
Hagar and viola! She conceives. Now Sarah has a new
problem. Her servant despises her. She is going to give the
master of the house something her mistress could not. I'm
sure in Hagar's mind her pregnancy should have elevated
her status within the household. To Sarah she was just

providing her one more service, like helping her dress or prepare the evening meal.

Sarah, like you and I, was only thinking in a physical, possible frame of thinking. The pressure made her forget the promise came from the God of the impossible. She forgot he doesn't break a promise, he doesn't lie, or that he hadn't set a time frame in which she would conceive, he only said she would. The truth of the matter is Sarah was never under any pressure to conceive, it was on God to keep his word.

Sarah's attempt to help God out caused issues between her and Abraham. In our scripture verse she placed all the blame for the situation between her and Hagar at Abraham's feet. Ishmael, Hagar's son was around 14 when Isaac was born. The generations of Ishmael became enemies to Israel and even today we are still fighting his descendants. Imagine if Sarah had never tried to help God. What would the world look like today? Would we be at constant war? I don't know. God never required Sarah's help because he had a plan and a time for Isaac to be born.

We all know God kept his word and when it was time, he told Abraham exactly when Sarah would conceive and what the baby's name would be. Every promise God has ever spoken he has brought to pass. If God has promised you something hang on to it. You may not see it today, tomorrow or in a year or five but if God said it, it's a promise.

QUESTIONS

1. Have you ever tried to help God out? How did that work out for you?

2. Why do we try to figure out solutions to the problems that overwhelm us?

3. What does it say about our level of faith when we pray, and then try to work it out?

4. Have you ever watched a friend struggle with a situation? They are praying on one hand but frantic about what they are going to do on the other. What advice did you give them? Were they wearing themselves out with the cares and concerns? It's different when we watch versus looking at ourselves.

5. Are you waiting on something now? Maybe God spoke a promise to you, or a word was prophesied over you. Are you trying to figure it out or are you trusting God and waiting on him and his timing?

REACTING TO THE STORM

LUKE 8:24

"They came to Jesus and woke Him up, saying, "Master, Master, we are perishing!" And He got up and rebuked the wind and the surging waves, and they stopped, and it became calm."

Jesus and the disciples were all on the boat. Jesus was sleeping while a huge storm was tossing the boat to and fro. Now Peter, James and John were all experienced fishermen, so they have been through storms on the water before. This storm must have been pretty bad for them to be feeling panicked and anxious. They finally wake up Jesus and he rebukes the winds and the waves; and it is smooth sailing from there.

THINK ON THIS...

On September 6, 2017 Hurricane Harvey had devastated Texas, Louisiana and it even flooded clear up into Nashville, TN. Barely a week later Hurricane Irma was heading towards Florida with Jose following close behind.

It got me to thinking of the three reactions people have to storms and how those reactions apply both physically and spiritually in our lives. How do you react when a storm is brewing in your life?

I learned in science and psych classes that there are two normal reactions: fight or flight. The third reaction I have found is "chasing". Have you ever heard of those people who chase storms? They call them *storm chasers* because they drive into hazardous conditions in order to watch tornadoes, hurricanes, and other storms. They snap pictures to show the power of a storm or fantastic lighting displays in the air. They have captured debris flying pass them or trees

23

swaying and bowing in the wind. Sometimes as Christians we run head long into circumstances and situations. We throw all caution to the wind. We haven't prayed about it, haven't sought any wise counsel, we simply jump in headfirst. Often times finding ourselves in over our heads. People have then drifted away, backslid or just plain walked away; because they think God failed them. Chasing a situation or storm in the physical or the spiritual is always hazardous. It can lead to death or injury. We should always count the cost; before facing a storm head on. How much are you willing to lose? What is there to gain? Is the gain worth the risk? Am I willing to lose my life over this?

The second group are those that choose "flight" in the face of a storm. The moment the word storm is mentioned they are packing their bags and loading up the car. Now in a physical storm, like a hurricane, there is some wisdom in choosing "flight". There are some storms we can't run from no matter how hard we try. No one has ever run from cancer, MS or diabetes. No matter where you go the storm is still with you. There is a stage people go through when dealing with death called denial. Mentally they try to run from the truth. They try to run away because the pain is so overwhelming. They run so they don't have to deal with those circumstances that are beyond their control. Spiritually, we try to run from God. We feel the tug and the drawing of his Spirit, but we run hard in the opposite direction. There is a misconception that living for Jesus is hard; but I have never found that to be true. We run when we feel convictions to change behaviors or attitudes. We run when God is asking us to step out by faith to start a ministry, to teach Sunday School, etc., etc., etc. Running is pretty much a time and energy waster. Especially when it comes to the things of God. The quicker we respond to God the faster peace will settle back over our lives. The quicker we respond to circumstances in the physical the quicker we can find peace of mind. Uncertainty keeps us awake at night and in constant turmoil.

Lastly, we come to the response of "fight". During hurricanes people insist on staying in their homes. People who are ill choose to do everything they can to get better and live. Sometimes these fights are to our detriment. During a hurricane you can't stop the wind, the debris from flying or the waters from rising. I can trust and believe God to protect me and my home though. I just need to listen to him and if he says "GO" guess what? I am gone! Spiritually, when tough times come, we fight by holding on to the promises of God. We speak those promises aloud. We don't allow anyone to rob us of what we know God can do. We might have moments of weakness, like David we whine a little, then we begin to reminisce and remind ourselves of other situations and times when God rescued us and saved the day. Before long the standard has been raised inside of us and we are once again standing. We have resumed our fighting stance; our hands are up and we are doing our fancy footwork to dodge the jabs of the enemy.

Every storm requires a different response. Every storm requires prayer in the spiritual realm and in the physical. It's not always wrong to chase, if no one ever chased nothing would ever change. Sometimes by faith you step out and what looks like a storm turns into a great watering of hopes and dreams. Flight allows you to stand and fight another day. Flight moves you out of the way of deadly storms and you live to see another day. Fighting is sometimes the only way to keep your head above the water. It is the only way to survive the storm. I'd like to say there is no wrong and no right answer; but the truth is in every storm there is a right way and a wrong way to approach it.

QUESTIONS

1. Write down a time when you were in a physical storm. Depending on where you live it might have been a blizzard, hurricane, tornado, earthquake or flooding. What type of storm was it? Did you chase it, take flight or fight it?

2. Did you make the right choice for handling that storm? Looking back was there a better option? If you had chosen another avenue, what would you have chosen? How do you think it would have turned out?

3. Can you think of a person in the bible who was in a storm and had to make a choice? Ex: Noah, Lot, Disciples, Paul. Who were they and what did they do?

4. Did the person you pick choose wisely or poorly in their method of taking on the storm? Pick one of the other 2 methods and tell how you think it would have turned out if they had chosen it. (It's ok to be creative)

5. We have talked about physical storms but what about a spiritual storm? How did you choose to face it? Looking back would you have handled it differently knowing what you know now?

LENS OF LOVE

1 Peter 4:8
"And above all things have fervent charity among yourselves: for charity shall cover the multitude of sins."

Peter is simply reminding us of the great sacrifice Christ made for us in this chapter. Therefore, we ought to live different, we ought not to do the things we once did and above everything else we ought to love others; because love (charity) forgives.

THINK ON THIS...
Love truly is blind. Love overlooks the flaws and foibles in each of our lives and in our character. True love knows you aren't perfect but somehow manages to overlook your shortcomings. Imagine if we could see past the flaws in every person we meet.

Think about that person you see in Walmart whose clothes look 2 sizes too small or who looks like they haven't showered in a couple of days. Our first thought is "ewwww" and then we wonder, "Did they look in the mirror before they left the house?" or "You could fry an egg on that head." We've all done it. We have all looked at other people and judged them by the outward appearance. We don't know them; we don't have any connection to them and our love for them is low. We have no idea what their back story is.

Maybe the person had to borrow clothes from a friend because their house and everything they owned burned up in it. Now they are in Walmart to buy a couple of new outfits, so they have something to wear. Maybe the unkempt, un-showered person has been holed up in a hospital room with a sick child and they are on their way home for a quick shower and a change of clothes but needed a few items to take home first. Love would have compassion and extend grace. It would offer a word of hello and work its way into a word of encouragement and prayer.

Love colors our vision. It isn't exactly the same as "rose colored glasses" syndrome, where you never see anything wrong or bad or negative. It's more like having corrective lenses. My glasses help me to see at different distances. Up close I actually see better without them on but for arms-length viewing and beyond everything becomes a blur without them. My glasses help me to see the smaller details, to see the whole picture if you will. Imagine if you looked at someone and all you saw was a blur. What if every time they made a mistake or hurt your feelings they became fuzzier, more blurred? One mistake too many and you wouldn't see them at all. They would become a blind spot in your vision. Like when you are driving, there is a certain place that is just outside of your vision even when looking in your mirrors. A car can be driving right next to you and you never see them. Thank God for love. Love knows the hang-ups, the issues and stills sees the good inside of us. It doesn't discount the negative points in our character; it just corrects our vision so we see the whole person more clearly. We appreciate every aspect, every circumstance that has shaped us into who we are.

Sometimes love allows people to love and care for you, when you can't stand to be around yourself. Love allows for someone to look at you and see how the flaw, the hurt in you is going to work for your good. That huge mistake you made is going to be the very thing that catapults you. Maybe it teaches you an important lesson or prunes away people you didn't need to be hanging with, maybe it helps you get some priorities straight in your life.

Love covers a multitude of sins. I know firsthand that this is true because of God's love for me. Jesus was born of a woman, made in the flesh...for us. Born to be the perfect lamb, the perfect sacrifice for my sins. Because of love Jesus willingly took a beating, was chastised and died on a cross to pay a debt I created and had no way of making restitution for. For the sole purpose that I might live and have ever lasting life. He looks on me and doesn't begrudge me what he suffered for me. He doesn't hold it against me. He only desires that I freely love him back and that I willingly leave behind the pleasures of sin to serve him and those around me. That I forgive others their sins and shortcomings just as he forgave me.

I am so thankful, grateful, humbled, in awe of my God who loves me so much. His love has covered over my multitude of sins to never be seen again and when he looks at me he doesn't remember them. He didn't just forgive me he wiped them out of his memory. No matter where I stumble or fall, he will never remind me of what a mess I have been or how I did this or that. All because of love.

QUESTIONS

1. Have you ever loved anybody despite their faults? Write about them. What were their faults?

2. Why is it easier to look past the faults and flaws of some people; yet we can't seem to see anything but the flaws in others?

3. Do you have any flaws, quirks or issues? What are they?

4. Do your flaws hinder you from being used by God? Do they really hinder you or are you hindered because you don't think you can be used?

5. Do you know everyone God used in the bible had a flaw or two? Moses stuttered and David was an adulterer. Yet we all know their names. List up to five other people in the bible and their flaws.

1.
2.
3.
4.
5.

SPOT THE DIFFERENCE

2 Corinthians 5:17
"Therefore if any man be in Christ, he is a new creature: old things are passed away; behold, all things are become new."

When we give our lives to Christ, we do so with a desire to be changed. As we grow in Christ people ought to see those changes manifested in us and strangers should look at us and know we are set apart, that we are different.

THINK ON THIS...
I have always enjoyed those "Spot The Difference" puzzles. You know the ones where you have two pictures? At first glance they look identical but upon closer inspection there are at least 6 differences between the two. Some of them you need to scour the picture, back and forth, up and down, side to side; they are not obvious at all. Other differences just seem to pop right out at you.

It got me to wondering. If we hung up two pictures side by side, one representing our life before we were saved and one that represented our current life, would people find any differences? Would your choice of beverage be different? Would your mode of dress be different? Would the attitude being portrayed have changed? What about the look in your eyes or your smile? Would your favorite radio station have changed? Oh, how about the jokes you laughed at and found funny? Perhaps the magazines you bought? What about the crowd you hung out with?

Can you honestly find differences in your life? I have to be honest. I am amazed at the differences in my life when I stop to think about it. I would love to tell you I got in church and everything changed overnight. I would be lying.

I had times of strong allegiance and times when I was falling out. Times when I was in church and still going to hell. I can't be any more honest than that. I look back on those times and it greatly grieves me; to know I grieved God. There came a day though when I told God I was all in. I was moving ahead with him and only him. That is when my picture changed dramatically.

I changed the crowd I ran with. The look in my eyes, my smile, my attitude all began to change. My priorities changed. My mode of dress has changed in subtle ways. I have to admit, when I am sitting in the church and a lady walks by whose dress only comes to mid-thigh and her cleavage is hanging out, I am embarrassed by her on one hand and saddened for her on the other. Saddened that she feels the need to gather attention in such a manner and embarrassed because she is showing off areas meant only for her husband's eyes. (She is also creating a stumbling block for some.)

Their picture hasn't changed yet. Modesty isn't a bondage, it's a matter of self-respect. Draw attention to you through your gifts and talents. Through your service and faithfulness to the house of God. They haven't learned there are better ways to draw attention or the lack of self-respect they are showing. It is simply an outward sign one can spot. A sign that shows whether or not a real change has taken place.

QUESTIONS

1. Can you see the importance of modesty for both men and women? On a personal level and in a group setting? Do you see how it could create a stumbling block for someone else?

2. Can you find 6 differences between your old and new pictures? I've started 2 columns here. Fill them in and add anything else you would like to include.

	Before	After
Favorite Hang out		
Favorite Drink		
Best Friend		

3. Is there a trait or attitude you are currently working on? What would you like to change? Do you think you have anything to work on? Why or why not?

4. Has anyone commented on how you've changed? Or asked why you don't go or do things you used to do? Write down comments or conversations.

5. Did you realize you had changed so much? If you haven't changed what is holding you back? What are you holding on to? More importantly, do you desire to change, even if you have already seen some change, to become more like Jesus?

AGREE

Acts 2:1

*"And when the day of Pentecost was fully come,
 they were all with one accord in one place."*

Jesus instructed those that were with him, before his
ascension, back in Acts 1:4. So here we are now 10 days
later. They are ALL together, ALL in one accord and ALL in
one place.

THINK ON THIS...

When is the last time you were trying to do something in
church, like planning a church outing, homecoming,
Christmas program and everybody was in one accord?

It's difficult enough to get two or three to agree on
something, let alone get a whole committee or congregation
on the same page. Yet in Acts 1:15, there were about 120
in the upper room doing just that. It's amazing to me there
were no debates over who they were waiting for or what
exactly this "Holy Ghost" is. No debates on how the Holy
Ghost would arrive, what it would look like or who could or
couldn't receive the power Jesus spoke about. Jesus said,
go tarry and wait for it. So, they did.

We need to strive to work together and work for the
common good. We have a tendency to hold our tongue, get
bent out of shape and fail to partake. We share with others
how we could have done things better, but of course, no one
would listen to us. We could have made the event more
effective or functional. I have to admit I have been guilty of
attending a function and finding fault. I have also run
events that didn't go exactly as planned and knew it could
have been better and learned from it. I know it is always
easier to look from the outside then to be in the middle of it.

We can't seem to work together on a simple fundraiser to send our children to camp. How will we ever come to the place of Acts 2:44-47? They sold their possessions - everything was common; it belonged to everyone as they had need. There was no yours and mine; today some married couples have separate bank accounts. In Acts, they were all on the same page, eating and living together with the purpose of sharing the love of Jesus and growing the church.

Go a little further to Acts 4:32-35. People are still working together, still in one accord and seeing thousands being added to the church. Imagine what we could do today if we worked together. How many could we save from the flames of Hell and add to the church?

What is happening within your church right now? Where could you join in and help? Is there a dinner coming up? A guest evangelist or singing group coming in? Is there a fund drive to raise money for camp or for a local agency?

Are you in charge of a committee or group within your church? Do you listen to others when they make suggestions? Do you incorporate other people's ideas? Do you allow others to help or take the lead?

This is a great skill to work on this week. Not only in church but at work and at home.

Questions?

1. Why is it so hard for people to come into agreement?

2. How can we funnel ideas, so everyone gets heard? So, everyone feels important and included?

3. Can you agree to disagree with others?   We don't always see eye to eye, but can you work on a compromise of ideas? Occasionally can you just say great idea and run with somebody else's thought?

4. Have you ever participated in any team building events or training? Tell about the exercise and what you feel made it successful.

5. Imagine you are the chairman of a big event. You have a group of 100 pastors coming to your church for a 2-day seminar. Using only the people in your study group or church (no more than 10 people) how would you organize them to get everything done efficiently? You need to do the following: Registration (Complete with welcome packages & name tags), Decorate the fellowship hall, serve danish and coffee each morning, lunch both days, have extra water and soft drinks available, ushers to direct your guests, and anything else you think is necessary. You have 30 days until they arrive. Who is on your team? What are their assigned tasks? What does your timeline look like?

I AM USEABLE

ISAIAH 30:14

*"And he shall break it as the breaking of the potters
vessel that is broken in pieces; he shall not spare:
so that there shall not be found in the bursting of
it a sherd to take fire from the hearth, or to take
water withal out of the pit."*

Today's scripture is part of a prophesy, but we are not going
to concentrate on the prophesy but the vessel itself. God
said it would be shattered to the point that it couldn't be
used to hold fire or to gather water. It was useless.

THINK ON THIS...

In the city there was a gate called The Potsherd Gate. It
was the place where all the broken pottery was discarded.
It was also the gate you went out to get down to the dump
where everything else was discarded and burned.
Everything outside of that gate was unusable, discarded,
unwanted and forgotten.

In the New Testament our bodies are referred to as "earthen
vessels" (2 Corinthians 4:7). Basically, we are clay pots
molded and fashioned by God's hand. 2 Timothy 2:20-21
says, *"But in a great house there are not only vessels of gold
and of silver, but also of wood and of earth; and some to
honour, and some to dishonor. If a man therefore purge
himself from these, he shall be a vessel unto honour,
sanctified, and meet for the master's use, and prepared unto
every good work."*

What type of vessel are you? I am always telling God I want
to be a vessel for everyday use. I'm not interested in being
the holiday gravy boat or platter. I'm not looking or
interested in being the main attraction a couple of times a
year. I want to be God's favorite go to dish or pot in his
kitchen. Or his favorite tool in the garage. That thing he
reaches for first without really giving it any thought. You

38

know the one, it's always within reach. It fits in your hand just right. You depend on it, it's perfect for all types of tasks. That is me or at least who I hope I am to God.

I want to be the one God looks for when he says, I need someone who will be honest and tell this person the truth in love...Amy! I need someone to sing this song so it can wash over my little lamb on Sunday morning who is struggling...Amy! Do you understand where I am coming from? I love to sing but I want to do it more than just for pageants and plays during Easter and Christmas. I want to be used in and out of the church. Use me in Wal-mart, use me in the restaurant, use me in the parking lot, use me, use me, use me! Here am I.

Do you truly want to be used daily? I am not concerned with what I am made of. Let me be wooden or aluminum or steel; I don't need to be silver or gold. I just need to be usable. I may have wear marks. I might be scuffed or scratched but I am still available and ready to go. I don't need to be polished and buffed; I need to be used of God.

I need to be ready, prepared for service at the drop of a hat. I need to be ready in season and out of season, I need to be ready when the pastor calls on me. I need to be ready when a friend calls and needs prayer, I need to be ready when the unexpected takes me by surprise, I need to be ready. I need to make everyday count. I need to be usable in the hand of the living God.

QUESTIONS

1. Are you serving or sitting on a shelf? If you're sitting on a shelf, why are you there? Who put you there?

2. Being usable means serving anywhere, to anyone you can. Meeting a need makes you usable. How have you been a usable vessel outside of church? What have you been doing?

3. Can you honestly say use me Lord? Anywhere, anytime, anyplace just use me. If you are saying "Yes" you had better be prepared. You might be in the grocery store or the auto parts place when God needs someone to pray or speak up.

4. Tell about someone you've prayed for, helped, or encouraged outside of the church. How were you usable in their lives?

5. So, what kind of vessel are you? Are you the holiday gravy boat or the favorite pan or tool? Are you content with the type of vessel you are? Explain which vessel you are like and why you feel that is what you are like. Are you happy with that or would you like more?

OWN WHAT IS YOURS

1 SAMUEL 17:38-39

"And Saul armed David with his armour, and he put an helmet of brass upon his head; also he armed him with a coat of mail. And David girded his sword upon his armour, and he assayed to go; for he had not proved it. And David said unto Saul, I cannot go with these; for I have not proved them. And David put them off him."

David was a young boy going out to do a man's job. So, Saul offers his personal armor, in an effort to protect him.

THINK ON THIS...

I imagine David looked like a 12-year-old trying to put on his dad's 3-piece suit. It hung on him, tripped him up and wasn't at all functional for him. Not to mention David had to deal with the weight of all that metal. 1 Samuel 9:2 says Saul stood a head and shoulders above all the other young men. He was very tall, and he was probably broad through his shoulders, yet he was expecting David to wear his armor. David wisely chose not to wear that which would weighed him down.

As we mature as Christians, we become convicted over certain behaviors, styles of clothing and so on. I have a friend who worked at Hooters when she was younger. She used her God given assets to her advantage to make great tips. Today she has convictions where her clothing is concerned. You will not find her in shorts and tank tops anymore. The very thought of wearing them is uncomfortable to her.

A conviction is more than a rule of thumb. There are churches that have strict dress codes or dietary restrictions. There are rules, rules the pastor or denomination feels are biblical and necessary. A conviction, however, is personal and I find it has to do with Godly growth. Sometimes rules can weigh a person down like Saul's armor did David. They can trip a person up causing them to stumble. Sometimes to the point of falling. When they fall, they are out of church and back to their old ways.

A conviction is not a weight. It isn't uncomfortable. It becomes a personal habit, a way of life. Doing anything else feels wrong. Don't get confused between a rule and a conviction. Obey the rules the Pastor puts before you as part of his flock. If they feel encumbering like Saul's armor, you may be in the wrong place. Seek God for direction and where he would have you to be. You may well be in the right place, sometimes God places us in uncomfortable circumstances in order to grow us or to be a help to someone else.

Own your own convictions from the Lord and don't try to put them on anyone else. Don't try to live convictions that aren't yours. Remember, convictions come from growing in God and forming godly attributes. They're part of our fruit. They grow out of our understanding for modesty, out of our understanding or desire to be surrounded in an atmosphere that is uplifting. Another couple, Randy and I went to support a local cafe. We have all become friends with the owners and often eat lunch there. That evening he was having some jazz music. We arrived well into the event and enjoyed some strawberry iced tea. Others were sipping on wine and it was a pleasant atmosphere until one couple decided to dance. The atmosphere changed and suddenly we weren't enjoying ourselves any more.

The atmosphere, like Saul's armor, was too heavy. It became uncomfortable and not a place we wanted to be in or an atmosphere we wanted to absorb. Being in ministry we are very cautious about the places we go and the things we do, you don't want "your good to be evil spoken of". (Romans 14:16)

Don't let anyone talk you out of your convictions.

QUESTIONS

1. Do you have any convictions? Any areas where you can't do the things you once did?

2. Have you ever felt suffocated by the rules or teachings of a church? What made you feel that way?

3. Looking back, do you think the rules or teachings of the church were right? As we mature in Christ, the things we once thought of as foolish we sometimes find to be wise later on. Explain your answer.

4. Can you see why one person's convictions are not necessarily meant for other people?

5. Do you think being in church is a conviction? If you miss church do you feel guilty? Do you put church ahead of everything else? (I know some jobs require Sundays) This is just your opinion. No right or wrong answer.

REVEALED

John 21:7
"Therefore that disciple whom Jesus loved saith unto
Peter, It is the Lord. Now when Simon Peter heard that
it was the Lord, he girt his fisher's coat unto him, (for
he was naked,) and did cast himself into the sea."

If you read the whole story, the disciples have been out
fishing all night and caught nothing. In the morning
someone yells from the shore asking if they have caught
anything and instructs them to throw their net back in on
the right. They comply and the net nearly breaks! It is
then, when John announces to Peter it's Jesus.

THINK ON THIS...
In the beginning of the chapter Peter says he is going
fishing. Fishing has always been his livelihood; until Jesus.
It's what happens at the end of the fishing trip that I want
you to catch.

Randy's dad is a commercial fisherman. If you don't know,
Randy is my awesome husband! His dad knows every place
mullet hide. (I personally do not like mullet. They have a
very strong taste. So, when they are eating mullet, it is my
pleasure to order pizza!) To me, Peter would have been like
Poppy, my father-in-law. He knew all the places to look and
all the tricks of the trade. Even the greatest fishermen have
a day when nothing works. Imagine being Peter and
someone from the shore says, "throw it in on the right and
you will get'em." Poppy would have grumbled and said,
"There ain't no fish on the right." Peter might have too. I
don't know how far they were from the shore; but it must
have been a little distance. After all, none of them
recognized who was shouting to them. I'm also pretty sure
the disciples were wondering how the man on shore was so
sure of himself. After all, they couldn't see any fish from
their position, and they were on the boat. Nevertheless,
they cast their net.

When they tried to pull the net back in, it was overflowing. Suddenly John had an epiphany. He realizes Jesus is standing on the shoreline and he TOLD Peter, "It is the Lord."

Sometimes circumstances work out for people and they don't realize it happened because of Jesus. You have to say to them, "Look what Jesus just did for you!" They hadn't caught a fish all night long, they are tired, hungry and discouraged. Not knowing what is happening or who is speaking they obeyed the command. For their troubles they got so many fish the boat was running over. If that isn't a blessing straight from Jesus what would you call it? Yet Peter didn't recognize where the blessing came from. When great things occur and people want to credit fate or chance or the universe, make sure you point Jesus out to them; so he gets all the glory and honor.

Pointing out the Jesus moments is a great way to witness. To let them know there is someone who will always have their back, if they will trust him. You give Jesus the glory and let them think on it.

QUESTIONS

1. When good things happen in your life are you simply amazed or do you thank Jesus for taking care of you? Do you recognize it was Jesus or do you think it was because your neighbor is a nice guy or you had over paid and you were due a refund?

2. Testify for a moment. Write about a time when it looked bad, but Jesus stepped in and it all worked out for you?

3. Have you ever had to point out the Jesus moment in someone's life? Did they recognize it when you showed them? Or shrug it off and credit karma and good vibes?

4. Do you have someone who will agree with you in prayer? You need to believe and agree with one another without doubting. Who is your second? If you don't who could you call? Tell why you chose them.

5. Have you ever read Matthew 5:45? It says, "That ye may be the children of your Father which is in heaven: for he maketh his sun to rise on the evil and on the good, and sendeth rain on the just and on the unjust." What does this scripture mean to you?

SUBDUE IT

GENESIS 1:28

"And God blessed them, and God said unto them, Be fruitful, and multiply, and replenish the earth, and subdue it: and have dominion over the fish of the sea, and over the fowl of the air, and over every living thing that moves on the earth."

God saw Adam's need for a companion and was moved with compassion. So, he has Adam consider each animal, naming every species. Upon finding none of them suitable, God created woman. He then gives Adam the keys to the earth so to speak. He gives him dominion to rule, maintain and keep order.

THINK ON THIS...

Imagine you have just seen and named every animal there is on the face of the earth. Now, you are responsible to keep the garden in order and above all don't eat from the Tree of the knowledge of Good and Evil (Genesis 1:17)

When you think about it, there where lions and tigers and bears, (Oh my!) in the garden with Adam. There were also gorillas, alligators, rhinos and other large animals with big scary teeth and horns. Maybe all the animals were leaf eaters in the garden; I don't know but they still had to look scary and even intimidating. It seems natural to me Adam would be more aware of them and concerned over their behavior than a small green garden snake that looks so inconspicuous.

Isn't that usually the way it works? Thunder is loud and scary, while the lightning flashes quietly and lights the darkness. Lightning giving you a glimpse of your surroundings; but lightning strikes quickly and can be very deadly. Sometimes those things that seem the most innocent, the last person you consider to be a threat, is the one that strikes you the hardest. They're like the car traveling in your blindside. They aren't hiding but they aren't in your scope of vision either.

We met a magician, who performs for large private corporate functions and Hollywood's finest, he said something I found very interesting. I'm paraphrasing here, he said you can do anything in front of someone and with the smallest distraction they will never know what you did. Mind you, he was talking about performing an illusion or using slight of hand, but I thought isn't that the way people get away with mischief? Men cheat with their wife's best friend and do it right in front of their wife's nose. The wife never suspects anything; because she trusts both of them. They love her and wouldn't hurt her, right?

The coral snake is small with lovely red, yellow and black rings. He isn't curled and rattling, his teeth and mouth are very small, yet he is deadly. Not every demon that bothers a soul is large; yet they cause one grief, doubt, discouragement, pity, fear, jealousy and the list goes on.

Be wary of your adversary and never discount the obvious. I know this is a different thought for today and not meant to make you suspicious of everyone you know. It is just a reminder to subdue the enemy and not to be surprised when you find out who the enemy is using to do his dirty work.

QUESTIONS

1. Are you a trusting soul? Do you give everyone the benefit of the doubt? Innocent until proven guilty so to speak.

2. Have you ever had anyone, who you thought was your friend or at least working on the same team; who totally undermined you? How did you handle it?

3. Can you or have you forgiven that person? Once you have forgiven them, does that mean you have to reinstate them as your friend or on your team? Do you have to trust them again?

4. As a parent, technically, we are meant to subdue our children. Have you ever thought of it that way? We are to teach, correct, and discipline them. Have you ever read your child's diary? Checked their devices to see who they're talking to or looking at? Do you know their friends? When they leave the house do you know exactly who, what, where and why? Is that invading your child's privacy? What are your thoughts.

5. Do you have an addiction? Chocolate, soda, coffee or soap operas. Maybe cigarettes, alcohol, drugs, or porn. Shouldn't we subdue our addictions? Let's be honest, addictions overtake us. Addictions control us. Anything that controls us, we have not subdued. How is your indulgence harming you? Is it harming those around you? Be honest and think about how you can subdue that thing which has control over you.

THINKING OF YOU

JEREMIAH 29:11
*"For I know the thoughts that I think toward you, saith
the Lord, thoughts of peace, and not of evil, to give
you an expected end."*

Jeremiah is prophesying here. God is saying I think of you
and I have plans for your life. I know it was said over in the
Old Testament, but it still applies!

THINK ON THIS...
You might be thinking that isn't how that verse goes. I
thought it said, "I know the plans I have for you." It does
say that in the NIV and other translations, but this is the
King James version (KJV), the closest you can get to the
original text in English. I like this version best because God
says he is thinking about me. The other versions sound like
he has made some plans and I'm a part of them. I just
think the KJV is more personal and it's a continual process.

God says, "I know the thoughts I think toward you". God is
sitting in heaven and thinking about me! He is thinking
specifically about you! David spoke of how God saw him in
his mother's womb. Take a moment to look up Psalm 139
and read verses 13-18. (It will only take a moment to pull it
up on your phone.) David understood how God saw him at
every stage of development. Before he was even complete
in his mother's womb, God saw him! God was thinking of
David as he was being formed! Just as he has done with
each of us. Saint or sinner; God has thoughts of each
person.

He knows what talents and abilities he has placed in each
one of us. He knows where he would like us to plug in, so
we reach our maximum potential and have the best life.
The scripture says he has plans for us of peace and not evil.
Don't we all want peace? Don't we all want to be happy and
have joy? Which of us says, I just want my life to be in

ruins so I can be miserable and make everyone else that way too? That's right, none of us.

Did you read Psalm 139? Did you notice in verse 17-18 what David said?
"How precious also are thy thoughts unto me, O God! How great is the sum of them! If I should count them, they are more in number than the sand; when I awake, I am still with thee."
David understood what Jeremiah would one day speak to the people. God's thoughts of you are more than the grains of sand! Have you ever been to the beach? More than all the sand you see. Imagine picking up a handful and letting it run through your fingers, for each one God has a thought of you!

Don't let anyone tell you, you aren't important. That is a flat lie of the devil. God said he is thinking of you and his thoughts are for peace. I like the last part too. God has an expected end for us. He is preparing us a mansion to spend eternity with him.

Just let that sink into your spirit today. You can't help but smile when you understand God is thinking about you.

QUESTIONS

1. Did you know God was thinking about you like that? That his thoughts of you are MORE than the grains of sand? How does that thought make you feel?

2. It seems like most of us are always searching for our purpose. We lament, "What am I here for? Where do I fit in? Well, what do you enjoy doing? What talents do you have? Cooking? Knitting? Volunteer? Work with children or seniors? Do you draw or like to build? Write down the things you love to do.

3. God will use those things you just listed for ministry. You don't have to search for your purpose. Your purpose is already a part of you. When you think back, can you find places your skills have already been used for ministry? What have you done?

4. Purpose does not come only when you step fully into position. It comes with every place you find to serve. Everything you do with your hands. Can you relate to that or find comfort in it? Let the anxiety go about your place and purpose?

5. What would you would love to do one day for Jesus? Would you like to write a book? Travel and minister? Teach Sunday School? Serve the homeless? What is the desire deep down inside of you?

AT ANY COST

Acts 16:3

*"Him would Paul have to go forth with him; and took
and circumcised him because of the Jews which were
in those quarters: for they knew all that his father was
a Greek."*

Paul liked Timothy and he wanted him to travel on with him
and Silas. His mother was a Jewess, but his father was a
Greek. Therefore, Timothy was not circumcised as the Jews
believed a man should be.

THINK ON THIS...

Sometimes, we do things not because it is necessary
according to the word but for the sake of our witness. For
this reason, Timothy was circumcised.

If a pastor requires men to wear a tie when they preach in
his church, guess what? Men wear a tie. It doesn't matter
how urgent you feel your message is for the the church;
without a tie they will never hear it. Whose fault is that?
Yours, for not wearing a tie and being obedient to the
pastor.

Obedience is better than sacrifice, I Samuel 15:22 declares
it. Refusing to wear a tie is rebellion. Which the very next
verse deals with, I Samuel 15:23, *"For rebellion is as the sin
of witchcraft, and stubbornness is as iniquity and idolatry."*
That is something to think about.

Sometimes, we must step outside of our own ideas and
comfort zones in order to maximize our witness. In this
walk, it is not always about us. Wearing a tie and being
obedient is a small price to pay to touch another person's
life. Timothy was willingly circumcised, so he could be an
effective witness for Christ to the Jews.

How far outside of your comfort zone are you willing to step? Would you do whatever it took? Are you willing? You might get asked to scrub the church bathrooms. Yes, that is a ministry. When visitors step into the facilities and everything is clean and sanitary it says a lot. If the facilities are dirty, people will think no one cares about the church itself and will probably not be back.

You might get asked to work in the nursery. Another very important ministry. You can pour into the children, but you are also allowing the parents to hear the word without distraction. As a young mother, I went to a church that didn't have a nursery. I had a great friend though. They would help me with the baby. I can remember many a service when I would have to leave the sanctuary because she was crying or needed to be changed. I missed a lot of the word in those days and I hadn't been a Christian very long. Somedays I wondered why I even tried to go but I was faithful and steadfast. Today I am so glad I was.

Whatever you are asked to do, do it with your whole heart. Do it without reservation, do it gladly and willingly. Your obedience could change a person's life for eternity. Don't be afraid to ask the Pastor, his wife or someone else with authority within the church where you can be of help. You could also look around you and see if you can identify a need. Think outside the box. Before implementing a big idea be sure to take it to the Pastor. Your Pastor should always know the ministries happening within his congregation so he can mentor, oversee and make sure everything lines up. Remember you are a reflection of your church and leadership.

Questions

1. Are you willing to do whatever it takes to share Jesus?

2. Are you willing to follow first? You have to start at the bottom and work your way up so to speak. First, you sit in the pew and listen. Then maybe you become an usher or sing in the choir, then you get to make announcements or sing a solo. Are you willing to follow first?

3. Are you willing to submit to church leadership? Willing to learn, observe or participate in training? Willing to report on what and how you are doing?

4. Are you willing to change your physical appearance if you are asked? There are some places where long hair on a man might not be received well. Are you willing to cut it? Make-up is taboo in some churches are you willing to scrub your face ladies? Or take your jewelry off?

5. Do you understand that our ways are not everybody's ways? We are always subject to the pastor and to his rules for the house of God he has been put over. Is it more important to have our own way or to be submissive for the sake of sharing the gospel?

DELAYED, NOT FORGOTTEN

ESTHER 6:3

"And the king said, What honour and dignity hath been done to Mordecai for this? Then said the king's servants that ministered unto him, There is nothing done for him."

The king couldn't sleep. Esther had held one banquet for him and Haman and they were set to have a second one. Something was disturbing him, so he had the book of chronicles brought out and read to him. It was like a kingdom diary, it recorded what was done and who done it and whether they received a reward or a punishment. Lo and behold Mordecai had thwarted a plan to kill the king and the king had not even acknowledged him, let alone reward him.

THINK ON THIS...

Have you ever felt overlooked? At work, at school, at home, by your friends or even at church? It's hard to imagine you're overlooked because God has something greater in mind than a mere thanks. What if that's precisely the reason? God's got something greater in the works; it could be.

It's not just in the area of thanks or appreciation where we feel overlooked at times. Imagine how Mary and Martha must have felt. Lazarus is dead and Jesus still tarries. Do you think it's possible they felt overlooked? I wonder if they felt a little anger, a little dismissed, a little unimportant where Jesus was concerned at that time? After all, Jesus said he loved them. So, where was he?

When God has a plan, we can't see it or imagine it in the midst of our trial. We never see it in the midst of the pain. We are looking around like blind men and all we see is the bleakness of our current circumstances. We are believing for Jesus to swoop in and save the day. We are looking for him to hear our call just like Superman would Lois Lane or the way Underdog heard Polly Purebred. We don't know from which direction Jesus will come or have a clue how he is going to get us out of this mess, this time. He always manages though, and he does it in such a way our feeble brain can't comprehend when it all comes together.

Isn't that precisely what Jesus did with Lazarus? He comes waltzing into town 4 days after Lazarus has died. By now the body is beginning to decompose, "he stinketh" is what they said. We are a lot like Martha, we believe Jesus can do anything and yet we limit him by what we speak and believe. Our carnal mind, our earthly thinking gets in the way. After all, Lazarus was dead, and he had been dead for 4 days.

Martha was having that very dialogue with Jesus, *"If you were here"* she said. She knew he could have healed her brother. *"He'll rise again in the resurrection of the last days...I believe..."* She knew one day she would see her brother again. She knew he would be risen in the resurrection. She missed what Jesus was saying to her though. Jesus said, *"I am the resurrection and the life..."* Jesus is still the resurrection and the life. He can still raise the dead and put life back in a body. Sometimes our faith wars with our mortal knowledge.

In the end, God had a plan. In our scripture today, it was Mordecai who had been forgotten. His action had been recorded and on this one particular night God needed the King to hear the account. In the middle of everything going on, I am sure Mordecai didn't foresee the king honoring him in such a fashion. Mordecai wasn't looking for recognition when he sent word to the king. He did however, save the kings life.
God had a plan concerning Mordecai and a plan for Lazarus as well. He even has a plan for you! Mordecai was given great recognition by the very man who sought to kill him. I love it when God makes your enemies a footstool for you.

"The LORD said unto my Lord, Sit thou at my right hand, until I make thine enemies thy footstool." Psalm 110:1
People may forget what you have done. They may not even recognize what you have done but God always sees and never forgets.

God raised Lazarus from the grave and there was nothing wrong with him. I bet he didn't smell a lick like death when he came out of that tomb. No effects of having been dead for 4 days, no weakness, no lingering signs of illness. He was whole and perfect.

God gets all the glory in every instance of our life. For every joyous, accomplished, delivered, revived, recognized, learned, moment we have; it is all due to his grace, his mercy and his divine hand.

Thank you, Lord, for seeing me this day. For knowing who I am, where I am and for having a purpose for my life. I surely love you Jesus.

QUESTIONS

1. Have you ever felt overlooked? Ever had an accomplishment go unnoticed? Have you been ready, able and felt qualified but someone else was chosen? What was your experience?

2. Did you ever feel overlooked, then from out of nowhere, someone congratulated you? Or a surprise was in the works the whole time and you didn't know it? Did you feel guilty for thinking no one remembered you?

3. Have you ever done something just because it was the right thing to do? Not because you were looking for compensation, not because anyone else was looking? What did you do?

4. Have you ever felt like God was late to meet your need? I try to remind myself I don't need it, until I need it. It isn't necessarily that God is late, we are just impatient. Was he late meeting your need, or did he come through right on time? Tell about it.

5. What do you think of this statement? There are times when we get delayed for our own good. Do you ever see how God is protecting you in those moments?

JABEZ

1 CHRONICLES 4:10

*"And Jabez called on the God of Israel, saying, Oh that
thou wouldest bless me indeed, and enlarge my coast,
and that thine hand might be with me, and that thou
wouldest keep me from evil, that it may not grieve me!
And God granted him that which he requested."*

Jabez had a desire to serve and to do it with God's help.
Even in his day, he realized, not everyone was going to be
on his side. He understood he would be tempted and tried
and he needed to be able to withstand the wiles of the
enemy.

THINK ON THIS...

You would think Christians would work together. Everyone
should be in one accord and everyone should have the same
objective. After all, isn't the point of ministry to help
someone else? To see a soul saved and a life changed? To
bring comfort to the heart or soul that is deeply wounded?
As a ministry, my husband Randy and I hold to this scripture
verse:

Isaiah 61:1
*"The Spirit of the Lord God is upon me; because
the Lord hath anointed me to preach good tidings unto
the meek; he hath sent me to bind up the
brokenhearted, to proclaim liberty to the captives, and
the opening of the prison to them that are bound;"*

Yet, we still pray the prayer of Jabez as we go. We have
been warned in the word to watch out for the wolves in
sheep's clothing (Matthew 7:15). We need to have spiritual
eyes to see beyond the skin of a man or woman. We say
beauty is only skin deep. The truth of the matter is, for
some, Christianity is only skin deep as well. It is like a
garment they put on when it suits them. When it benefits
them, they are a Christian, but in those other times watch

out because they will chew you up and spit you out without a second thought.

I have heard several people express the thought about life being simpler when they sat in the pew and simply worshipped God. They found when they began to work behind the scenes, people in leadership were not always what they had perceived them to be. They discovered true personalities of the people they had only seen on the platform. They learned aspects of the church they had never known sitting on the pew and not being a part of church leadership. Again, pastors and leaders are just people. We are all prone to anger on occasion or to bad judgement. We need to check ourselves, make sure we aren't coming to worship the pastor instead of God.

I often think of Elijah fearing for his life when Jezebel came after him. He thought he was all alone. It was then, when God reassured him there were still 7,000 who had never bowed down to Baal. Sometimes, in this walk, it is very easy to feel alone. It's during this time when you realize just how many wolves there truly are among you.

I refuse to be one of them! How about you? I refuse to use people. I refuse to let my walk be affected by others who choose to half-heartedly serve and give of themselves. I choose to surround myself with people that choose God above all else. People who think like me, desire a walk like me. People who know who God is, what he will do and trust him to the very core of their being.

I pray the prayer of Jabez today. God enlarge our borders, please. Let us reach more souls for you. Let people see in us nothing but Jesus and know the sincerity of our testimonies and lives. Protect us from the evil that threatens on every side and don't let it overtake us or harm us. I bless your holy name and I thank you for the journey. In Jesus name. Amen.

QUESTIONS

1. Have you ever been disillusioned by someone you held in high esteem? Inside the church or out, saint or sinner, what was your initial impression of them and what changed that opinion?

2. Do you think your life, your walk has ever left anyone disillusioned about who you are? What did they see that changed their opinion of you? Was it justified?

3. Can you see the wolves around you? John 10:12 talks about the hireling. A pastor (today it would also refer to a musician or singer) who is only in it for the money. You might see it in the congregation as well. People who are only looking for dates or trying to sell a product. What do you see?

4. Why are you in church? Really, why are you in church?
   What are you looking to get out of it? What are you
   putting into it?

5. Are you looking for your territory to be enlarged? Or
   make a greater impact? In what way would you like to
   expand?

NEVER ENOUGH

2 SAMUEL 12:8

"And I gave thee thy master's house, and thy master's wives into thy bosom, and gave thee the house of Israel and of Judah; and if that had been too little, I would moreover have given unto thee such and such things."

God has sent Nathan the prophet to rebuke King David for his multiple sins. He lusted, he committed adultery, he tried to cover it up and he had multiple people killed to remove the one person he needed out of the picture.

THINK ON THIS...

David had it all. He had numerous wives/concubines and children, servants, lands, cattle, sheep, goats, camels, donkeys, gold, silver, you name it and he had it. Yet somehow enough is never enough for us.

God in all his glory told David, if what he already had was TOO little, he would have given him more! That is just a paraphrase of our scripture today but think about it. We have already recounted everything David had, and God says, *"if it had been TOO little."* Put it in a more personal context. For me, God was saying, *"Amy, if what you have is TOO little, ask me and I will give you more!"*

The more I thought about it, the more overwhelmed I became. There are things Randy and I are desiring. Personal things and things for ministry. Sometimes we feel like maybe we are asking for TOO much. When you are pleasing to God though, it pleases God to indulge you. When our children are well-behaved and are pleasing to us, it pleases us to indulge them. We are God's children.

I began to think of everything God has already given us. Every time he has kept us safe and protected us. I thought about the many blessings he has already poured out on us.

How he provided our current bus (RV), how he has paid for repairs and travels and other expenses. How he has put people in our path who love on us and bless us. Then I hear him saying, "If it is TOO little, I will give you more."

In the midst of being overwhelmed, tears streaming down my face, I acknowledge he has given us much and make my requests known for what we have need of. Knowing what the word says, knowing all the promises of provision, knowing that he is faithful, knowing, knowing, knowing and feeling the absolute fullness of his blessings in my life.

What is it you have need of? What is it you truly desire? Have the full assurance today, if you are pleasing to God it is his desire to indulge you. (Just be sure you don't ask amiss. Don't ask for sinful, spiteful, malicious things. Ask for blessings.)

QUESTIONS

1. Do you believe, truly believe, God will give you more than you already have?

2. Can you testify about a time when you had a need and you prayed with all your heart believing God and he moved? What did he do for you?

3. Do you thank God for what you already have? Better yet, have you even taken stock of what you already have? List it out right here. You might have an old beater car; but it gets you from a to b. Thank you, Jesus! I bet you have more than you realize. I left you lots of room to list your blessings.

4. How do you feel right now? When you look at this list and see all that you have? Did you list your parents? Siblings? Did you list everything? Look again. Imagine God calling your name and saying, "If it is TOO little, I will give you more." Honestly, you ought to be overwhelmed.

5. Are you faithful like David? Yes, he slipped, he made several horrible mistakes and paid for it; but he also repented. By tithing, taking care of the church, you create the atmosphere for God to meet all of your needs. Then your faithfulness, your obedience, your love of Him creates the atmosphere where he asks, "if it is TOO little." Do you meet these requirements? If you answered yes, write what it is you need. Be specific! God is all about the details. Oh, and be honest. Don't ask for a big SUV if you can't afford the insurance and the gas for it. Because God knows and he will wait for you to get real with him.

PEER PRESSURE

Mark 6:26
"And the king was exceeding sorry; yet for his oath's sake, and for their sakes which sat with him, he would not reject her.

King Herod has John the Baptist locked in prison. John spoke the truth about his relationship with Herodias, his wife, who had been his brother's wife. This greatly angered Herodias and she desired to see John dead in retaliation.

THINK ON THIS...
There are several instances in the word where people, men of great stature really, caved in under peer pressure. Afraid of what their friends or colleagues would think or do if they failed to follow through. If they chose to do the right thing instead of the popular one. Afraid to admit they had made a mistake or spoken too hastily.

See it was Herod's birthday, the daughter of Herodias came in and danced for him in front of all his guests. In his great delight Herod offers her anything she wants, up to half of the kingdom. He doesn't think of the possible consequences his words might cause. She inquires of her mother for the thing she should ask for. Herodias wants John the Baptist's head upon a platter and so it was.

The problem was, Herod offered it in front of his peers, Lords, Noblemen, etc. Now he feels obliged and stuck. The true measure of any person is the ability to do what is right. I wonder what would have happened if he had replied with something like, "I will *give* you anything, but I cannot *take* a life." It changes the perspective.

The other problem that usually occurs in these instances is remorse. Herod knew John personally. The bible says in verse 20,
"For Herod feared John, knowing that he was a just

man and an holy, and observed him; and when he
heard him, he did many things, and heard him gladly."

King Darius was in the same position when he threw Daniel in the Lion's Den. He made a decree after his advisors puffed up his ego. When he realized how they had manipulated him. When he realized their intent was to remove Daniel permanently, the king prayed and could not sleep. We know it all worked out. Daniel was alive in the morning and the King declared that Daniel's God was the true and living God. It all came about though, because the king caved under peer pressure.

What about when King Xerxes summoned Queen Vashti? He wanted to show her off like a prized possession to all his drunken cronies. She refused him. He was embarrassed and in the heat of the moment he listened to his consultants. The problem was they really weren't concerned with his issue. They were concerned with their wives and the possibility of being refused by them. In this instance, God used Xerxes mistake to save the Jewish people. Queen Vashti however, received consequences that changed her life forever. She was stripped of her title and was never allowed before the king again.

Peer pressure is a real problem. It takes a strong person to admit they spoke too hastily or spoke without really considering the consequences or possible ramifications. Sometimes we just need to own up to our own flaws and shortcomings. To our fits of anger and outbursts.

QUESTIONS

1. Have you ever had to eat your own words? Put up or shut up? Did you cave to your peers or stand up for what was right?

2. If the men we talked about today had stood up and said "No" what do you think would have happened to them? They were all leaders, the top of the food chain, what possible consequences do you think they might have faced?

3. Today, if a leader would stand up and admit, "I made a mistake". Do you think people would forgive them? Would you? Think about leaders in your lifetime that have made mistakes, who followed along with their party and cronies? Name one of them, what did they do? Do you think things would have turned out different if they took responsibility and sincerely apologized?

4. Let's make it more personal. Every Friday, co-workers go to the corner pub for drinks and wings. One Friday you go. You have a coke and a few wings before heading home. One week turns to two, which turns into a month and soon every Friday you are at the pub. Someone buys you a beer, instead of saying thanks but no thanks you think it's only one beer. It'll be ok. Now you are not only going to the pub but that one beer has led to several every week. A few games of pool, some harmless flirting. It's all gotten out of hand. Friday is coming, everyone is talking about it; including your spouse. What do you do?

5. How do we teach our children to stand up to peer
   pressure? Do you have a story of how you helped your
   children or how your parents helped you? Write it down

STUFFY TRADITIONS

Mark 7:9

"And he said unto them, Full well ye reject the commandment of God, that ye may keep your own tradition."

Jesus is speaking to the Pharisees here. They are concerned with traditions and things that are lawful according to man but not necessarily according to God.

THINK ON THIS...

King Solomon declared there is nothing new under the sun and how right he was. Even in the 21st century with all of our technology and so-called intelligence we still behave badly and many still lack the understanding of this verse.

There are those who think the things they do outwardly make them godly. Like the Pharisees washing their hands before they eat or lengthening the hem of their garments. Those things only affect how you look and can cause you to judge others. If you didn't wash your hands before eating, the Pharisee's basically declared you a backslider. Heaven forbid your garment only went to your knees; theirs went clear to their ankles.

In some traditional churches, many have been taught the gifts of 1 Corinthians 12 are no longer in effect, especially the gift of tongues. Teaching it is only given to some, if it is given at all; and then only if there is someone to interpret. I wonder what Jesus would say to them.

Just because an elder, pastor, or parent says a scripture means this or that does not mean you shouldn't search it out for yourself. They only know what they have been taught. I often think of Aquila and Priscilla and how they took Apollos aside.

Acts 18:26

"And he (Apollos) began to speak boldly in the

synagogue: whom when Aquila and Priscilla had heard, they took him unto them, and expounded unto him the way of God more perfectly."

Apollos could have rejected what they said to him because of his traditions. That wasn't what his pastor, parents and leaders had taught him. Those teachings were good enough for all of them, therefore it's good enough for him. What more did he possibly need to know? Have you ever heard anyone say that? I have. We need to be teachable, humble, willing to listen. We don't want to miss God when he is trying to instruct us so we can grow.

Study it out, if the word is different than what you have been taught or understood, then pray and ask God for wisdom, knowledge and understanding. You may have to ask for days or weeks on end, but God will answer you. He wants you to know what is right and what is wrong. Understanding the gift of tongues is extremely difficult for some. The main reason many won't hear and believe, is due to the traditions or teachings of the church. They simply haven't experienced it. I challenge each of you to go back and search out the gift again and to pray about it. It is the greatest gift, right after salvation, you can ever receive this side of heaven.

Which traditions in your life are holding you back? Which traditions cause you to judge others? A tradition is something you do because it's been passed down from generation to generation. In my family, we have a cookie recipe that has been passed down. We make them at Christmas. A simple rolled out recipe we bake and decorate. But oh, how we look forward to them. Traditions can be a great thing; or they can be something that hinders and stifles you.

Remember, this whole study is called **Think On This**. It's sole purpose is to stretch you, your thinking, your walk, what you believe, everything you know or think you know. I challenge you to read Mark 7 and to ask God if there are any doctrines of man, any traditions you are holding on to, that are contrary to his word. There is nothing wrong with a tradition; unless it's holding you back from everything God has for you.

QUESTIONS

1. Do you have a tradition in your family that everyone looks forward to? What is it and why is it so special?

2. Are there any traditional thoughts in your family you disagree with? It might racial, political, educational or a million other things. Write down the traditional thought and how you see it.

3. Read 1 Corinthians 12, what are your thoughts about the gifts of the Spirit. Do you think they are all still available and in operation today?

4. Have you ever seen any of these gifts in operation at your church? i.e. Does anyone speak in tongues? Have you heard a message interpreted? Have you ever heard a word of knowledge spoken?

5. If you have never experienced or been taught about the gifts, can you consider with an open mind and read it again? Can you look past the traditional teaching to the possibilities? Remember what Joel prophesied? He said in the last days God would pour out his Spirit upon all flesh. He said your sons and daughters would prophesy. Your young men would see visions and old men would dream dreams. Aren't we in the last days? What are your thoughts, your thoughts, not the standard answers you learned; but your own thoughts concerning what the scripture says.

THE WAY OF MATURING

GALATIANS 4:4-5
"And beside this, giving all diligence, add to your faith virtue; and to virtue knowledge; and to knowledge temperance; and to temperance patience; and to patience godliness; and to godliness brotherly kindness; and to brotherly kindness charity."

Paul is writing to the church in this epistle or letter. He is instructing them on the things they should be doing with all diligence to grow and mature in Christ. He is also writing to us.

THINK ON THIS...
I was recently part of a weekend filled with Christians. I was with fellow laborers who are preaching and singing to share Christ. Now, I'm not perfect by any means, ask my family. I have flaws and areas where I am still working out my own soul salvation. I'm still praying. Still asking God to shape me, mold me, scrap me or whatever it takes to make me who he has called me to be.

That being said, it pained my spirit at some of the things I heard others saying. I'm going to paraphrase, as I can't remember the exact words, but you will understand the point of this comment. "We need to stop pointing fingers at the sin of the gay choir director or the pianist who's sleeping with the deacon because we all have some secret sin we are trying to hide. Theirs is just out in the open where everyone can see it." Do you see anything wrong with that statement?

From my stance, I see the platform as the Holy of Holies. It is the most sacred place. It is the place where those consecrated for service stand. It is the place where we look, as Christians, for an example of how we ought to live, talk and walk. In the tabernacle, only the High Priest went in and he ONLY went once a year to meet with God. He had to be above reproach in every aspect of his life. If he were gay, adulterous, a drunkard, a liar, or a thief he would have been dead on the spot and they would have had to drag his dead body out of the room!

Let me ask you a question. Did the gay choir director or the deacon repent of their sins? If they did, why are they still living a lifestyle that is clearly an abomination in the eyes of God? Are they truly saved? Should they die right now would they hear Jesus say, "Well done my good and faithful servant enter in"? I'm not asking you to be their judge; I'm just posing a question. I'm using the examples spoken by the person above that vexed my spirit. I want you to think about it. I'm not saying don't love or be concerned about them, I'm asking about their sin. Differentiate between the two; its important.

I am not suggesting one sin is greater or that there are degrees of sin in the eyes of God. Not by any means, shape or form. I just want you to consider something and let it roll around in your thinking for a couple of days. True repentance means I turn 180 degrees from what I was doing and act the complete opposite. If I was a drunkard, I am now sober. If I was a thief, I now pay my own way. If I was gay, I am now straight. If I was unfaithful (adulterous), I am now old faithful.

If sin is still rampant in your life, the platform is not the place for you in church; the pew is. Those on the platform are striving to grow and mature in Christ. Their walk is solid and at any time they find their walk to have slid backwards, it is time to step down and sit on the pew for a while. Better to admit our failures and to set ourselves down; then to be found out and cause others to stumble.

Let's go back to our scripture verse for today because there are other areas of our life we need to work on after repentance. For example, the word says to be angry and sin not. We all get angry, we all become disgruntled, so how do

81

we sin not? First and fore most we repent. Then we add to our faith, virtue.

Virtue is morals, it's standing firm in what we believe. We then add to that knowledge. We read the word and we ask questions. The bible says to seek out wise counsel. Go ask an elder or pastor, ask someone whom you know understands the word and how to apply it. Then add some temperance. Understand you are not in control of everything and let go of the stuff you can't change. Add some patience. Don't you hate that word? Somethings in life we just can't change. Like standing in line, only there is a new cashier. The line is 10 people deep and people are grumbling; I am going to wait my turn and smile. Patience may not be something I like or manage to exhibit all the time but I'm going to work on it and move on. Add godliness. Show Christ while you are standing there. While others are grumbling remind them, we all have to learn. Smile at them, ask how their day is going. Use it as a time to minister to those around you. Maybe God put you in that line because the person behind you needs prayer. That slides us into brotherly kindness. Perhaps the person behind you is running extremely late and you let them ahead of you or you pay for their items. Add charity. Do it all in love.

God loves you and he wants the best for you. Start with faith and add to it until you simply love people.

QUESTIONS

1. What are your thoughts about a person, openly living in sin, being allowed on the platform? Are you ok with that? Why or why not?

2. When a pastor, deacon or elder is having an affair with the piano player what is the message being sent to everyone in the pew?

3. Should we pay people to play on the worship team? Keeping in mind, they aren't church members; they don't claim to be saved. Most Sundays they play and leave before the preaching starts. However, on Friday & Saturday night they play at a local bar. Yes, there are church members who play, just not as well. What is the message when we pay musicians? Do you think they will get saved or will they pull others out of church and into the bar?

4. Christian living is like building with Legos or Lincoln Logs. You have to create a foundation to build on. Do you see the importance of building up your walk with Christ before you stand in a place of authority and position in the church?

5. Do your feel the pulpit and platform are as important today as the Holy of Holies was in the days of Moses? Explain your thoughts.

WHAT DID I DO WRONG

2 Samuel 11:11
"And Uriah said to David, "The ark and Israel and Judah are dwelling in tents, and my lord Joab and the servants of my lord are encamped in the open fields. Shall I then go to my house to eat and drink, and to lie with my wife? As you live, and as your soul lives, I will not do this thing."

Uriah was a soldier in David's army. He was being honorable in this verse. He was trying hard to do the right thing. Sometimes you can do everything right and still get the short end of the stick.

THINK ON THIS...
David went up on the roof, at a time of day he knew should be off limits to him. It was the time of day when the women would go up to bathe. Temptation drew him and he just rode the wave.

From his rooftop he gazed upon Bathsheba, Uriah's wife. Yet temptation drew him again and again and he just rode the wave. One sin led to another sin. First, he watched her from a distance. When he should have repented and left it alone, he rode the wave and dove straight into another sin by inviting her to his house. Another wave crashed when he seduced her, another sin committed.

Now, in today's world our first thought is, she didn't tell him no. She didn't run away or fight or do anything. So she is just as guilty as he is. But if I go back to the story of Esther, I realize kings had the power of life and death. Approach without being asked and if the scepter isn't extended, guess what, you're dead. The king got whatever the king wanted, when he wanted it and he wanted Bathsheba.

Those few waves led to Bathsheba carrying King David's child. It must be David's child because poor Uriah has been out fighting with the king's army. Uriah is gone putting his life on the line for his country and his king. What's his king doing for him?

Temptation knocks on David's door again. A whole new set of waves are set to carry the king farther than where he can safely swim. He has committed adultery and the proof will soon be showing itself. Attempting to cover his sin, he rides the wave. He calls for Uriah to be sent to him. David is so clever, what man wouldn't jump at the chance to come off the battlefield? Especially when it means he can spend the night with his wife?

But here comes faithful, loyal Uriah. The king says, get a good nights sleep and see me in the morning. You can almost hear David kind of chuckling to himself, thinking the poor sap will never know when that baby comes that it isn't his. He will be over the moon and no one will be any the wiser. He was giddy and well pleased with himself. Morning comes shedding a new light on his devious deception. David realizes Uriah has slept on the King's doorstep all night with the rest of his servants!

David is bewildered. Why on earth wouldn't Uriah go home to his comfortable bed, to his beautiful wife and enjoy the opportunity given to him? Read our scripture again for Uriah's reply. Uriah was being faithful and thoughtful of his fellow soldiers. He was still on duty.

So now David is a little desperate. The wave is cresting higher and he keeps Uriah with him for another night. Plying him with wine to get him drunk. Surely, he will not be thinking clearly. Surely, Uriah will go straight home to his wife. But when the dawn breaks, David rushes to look, there among the servants of David's house is Uriah.

The wave is great now, like the kind hurricanes produce. Desperation has created a thin perspiration upon his lip, David is frantic as he writes a letter to Joab, his chief in command over the army. One small wave standing in the shallow waters has carried David so far out his feet can no longer touch the bottom. Sheer panic has set in and David rides a wave that breaks underneath him. He orders Uriah to be placed on the front line of the most heated battle available. He further writes to withdraw those around Uriah. David basically said to push Uriah to the forefront to ensure his death. Then David dispatches the letter of execution; sending it with Uriah! Uriah has no idea what words are contained within the letter he carries to Joab.

Joab, as commanded, places Uriah in the worse battle there is. He puts him on the front line and before the day is over Uriah is dead. One more wave, one more coverup, and David thinks he is home free. David marries Bathsheba as the mourning period is over and believes his sins are hidden forever; no one will ever know what he has done.

As the story continues to unfold the baby is born but he is very ill. David fasts and weeps for the child, praying God will spare him. David's sin has caught up with him. It costs him the life of his child.

David and Bathsheba go on to have Solomon who was the richest and wisest to ever live. It never says they lived happily ever after. Bathsheba, Uriah and the baby all suffered consequences because of David's actions. They did nothing wrong. Uriah died not knowing what happened in secret. An innocent child died and Bathsheba lost her husband and baby.
Bad things happen and it isn't always because of something we did. It's good to evaluate where you are and make sure you are walking on solid ground and on the right path. Where good is, evil is present.

QUESTIONS

1. Have you ever suffered a consequence because of someone else's actions? What did they do and how did it affect you?

2. Let's reverse that first question. Have your actions ever caused someone else to suffer consequences? What did you do and how did it affect them?

3. Have you ever done something you shouldn't have, like David, and one wrong action led to another and another? Tell the sequence of events and how it all ended.

4. Let's look at David's story, it's easy to see how one wrong move can cause everything to spiral out of control. Many people have fallen out in big ways because of one indiscretion, one lie, or one wrong turn. Can you think of anyone in history who fell from grace because they made one mistake that led to big problems? (It can be American history or from any part of the world.) Who was it and what happened?

5. How can we keep things from spiraling out of control? How do we keep from going from one mistake to another?

LANDMARKS

PROVERBS 22:28
*"Remove not the ancient landmark, which thy
fathers have set."*

In the Old Testament we read where the men would take
stones to create landmarks. God instructed them to teach
their children of the significant events that happened in that
place when they came upon them in their travels.

THINK ON THIS...
It seems in the 21st Century landmarks do not have the
same significance they once did. Anti-Christian groups have
worked hard to see crosses and 10 Commandment statues
removed from across the country. In 2017, we saw them
remove civil war statues because they offended people. You
can remove all the landmarks you want but it doesn't change
the history that has made America who or what it is.

Landmarks have a great historical value. It reminds us of
where we have come from, how we have grown, of the
people who fought for our rights and freedoms. When we
remove them, we make their sacrifices of no importance.
Every man who fought in the Civil War had a family he left
behind to stand for what he believed in. Many died or were
wounded in combat. That war brought the North and South
together; otherwise we might still be at odds with one
another. It brought an end to slavery; it changed the whole
trajectory of our country. All these years later, people are
offended over history?

We have personal landmarks as well. Isn't that why we
celebrate birthdays and anniversaries? We have landmarks
or memories of moments or events that changed and
shaped our lives. When my daughter was just 15 days from
turning a year old, we were robbed in our home. My head
still bears the scars from being hit with a punch can opener I
used to open her formula. Those scars are a landmark. We

purchase souvenirs when we travel, we buy class rings and yearbooks in school, we have pictures taken or grab snapshots to remember special moments or to mark growth. As Christians we get baptized and record the date. Not every landmark is a happy one. We have landmarks that represent divorce, death, and other heartbreak. Which landmark in your life would you choose to remove? Everyone one has added or removed from your life to create who you are today.

Some landmarks are hard to look back on, but I wouldn't choose to remove it. If I removed the landmark of my grandmother's death because it was so painful, wouldn't I then have to remove every landmark of my grandmother from my life? Otherwise I have a missing grandmother from my life's story with no reason for her removal. Her death though and the illness that preceded it changed me. I no longer wanted to be a nurse. I had seen a whole different side of it. Her illness is what started me praying and her death is what caused me to draw closer to Jesus. Her death, though painful, was a huge landmark in my life and in who I have become.

Don't be in a hurry to remove landmarks. Whether they are historical or personal. Each one is erected for a purpose. Each one tells a story that is significant in its own way. Enjoy your landmarks, even the ones where you shake your head and ask yourself, "What was I thinking?" Mistakes help us to move, to grow, to change and mature. As a matter of fact, take some time to look over your landmarks and see how much you have learned, how much you have changed. Thank God for every landmark, even the stupid ones. :0)

QUESTIONS

1. I agree there are certain situations in our life we wish we could "do over". People say I would like to be 20 again but only if I knew what I know now. We know it now because of those situations. Can you name 3 landmarks in your life?

   1.

   2.

   3.

2. Let's look at the first one you listed. Approximately how old were you when this happened? Describe how it changed you. Was it a good change or a bad change? Did you learn anything from it?

3. Same thing. What about your 2nd landmark? Approximately how old were you when this happened? Describe how it changed you. Was it a good change or a bad change? Did you learn anything from it?

4. Yep, same drill, tell about Landmark number3. Approximately how old were you when this happened? Describe how it changed you. Was it a good change or a bad change? Did you learn anything from it?

5. Would you remove any of these from your life? If you did which one would you remove? What other memories, landmarks or events past or future would you have to remove? Remember, every landmark has a ripple effect that travels in all directions. To totally eradicate the landmark from your life everything associated with it has to be changed or removed.

CHARACTERISTICS

GALATIANS 5:22-23
"But the fruit of the Spirit is love, joy, peace, longsuffering, gentleness, goodness, faith, meekness, temperance: against such there is not law."

In Psalms 8:5 it says, and I am paraphrasing here, we were made a little lower than the angels but in the original Hebrew it says we were made a little lower than Elohim. A little lower than God himself. Hence, we are created in His image not the image of the angels, which are created beings.

THINK ON THIS...
There are a lot of facets about us that mirror God. It says in John 5:7, "For there are three that bear record in heaven, The Father, The Word and The Holy Ghost: and these three are one." In Isaiah 11:2 we also find the seven spirits of God, which are the Spirit of: The Lord, Wisdom, Understanding, Counsel, Strength, Knowledge and Fear of the Lord. All this makes up His image.

Personally, I am a daughter, wife and mother. God is a Father, Son and Spirit. I am looked to at times for wise counsel. I use wisdom, I have strength gained through faith. I have knowledge to apply the word of God. I have common sense and I have a fear of the Lord, who has the power to send my soul to Hell. I also understand spiritual things and have a power within me that is fully God. I am created in His image.

Growing up I learned valuable lessons and skills from my mom. I learned by imitating her and watching how she reacted and responded to varying circumstances. Her views and thoughts colored my views and thoughts growing up. I learned respect, manners and hospitality at her side. When I became a Christian, I learned at the feet of my Jesus. I learned greater depths of forgiveness, giving, and compassion. I learned I had more strength to stand, more wisdom to advise and a true well of knowledge to draw on.

Regardless of who I used to be. Regardless of my past mistakes, failings or misgivings. I am not that person any longer. I may have cracked, damaged, even broke who I was originally created to be, but when I sought Jesus, he healed all those affected areas. Did you know, if you break a bone it becomes stronger in that area? So, we become stronger in all those areas Jesus heals with his love. Don't pick at the scab. Don't keep reminding yourself of how bad it was. Allow yourself to move forward and to become whole.

In becoming whole we find our true identity. We begin to mirror the attitudes Jesus modeled for us. We begin to imitate and strive to achieve the fruits of the Spirit mentioned in our scripture. With each endeavor we leave our old selves behind and walk into the characteristics God intended for us in the beginning.

We may not become the exact vessel or type of vessel as God originally intended. Instead, we become a vessel of greater character and strength because of the trials we have been through. God reshapes, remolds, re-glazes, re-fires us. He sands us and goes through some of the processes again. To make us a useable vessel in his hand.

Don't despise the bumps or hard places you've had in your walk. God is using those places to sand you, to scrape and fire you. Every trial, every circumstance is bringing out the best you he can create. Thank him and keep walking.

QUESTIONS

1. Do you have past mistakes you're still beating yourself up over? What are they? Be specific. (You don't have to share everything if you are in a group study.)

2. Are you still making the same mistakes? If yes, why? If no, why not? How does that answer make you feel about yourself today?

3. Have you ever used your past mistakes in order to witness? Without those mistakes, would your witness have been as effective?

4. When you repented, you asked God to forgive you of all your past mistakes. But have you forgiven yourself? Have you asked yourself for forgiveness? Did you actually speak it out loud? If not, could you? Try it? Did you forgive yourself?

5. Take a moment and write down who you are in Jesus. Write down the qualities you have that mirror God. When you forget who you are, when you are plagued by your past, come back here and be reminded of who you are today.

FRUITFUL OR FRUITLESS EFFORTS

John 21:3

"Simon Peter saith unto them, I go a fishing. They say unto him, we also go with thee. They went forth, and entered into a ship immediately; and that night they caught nothing."

The chapter says seven of the disciples are together on the shore of Tiberias and Peter decides he is going fishing. The other six all choose to follow after Peter and jump into the boat.

THINK ON THIS...

Peter may have been the rock on which the church was built but like all of us Peter learned things the hard way. Peter was a natural leader. He decides to do something, and the other disciples jump up to follow him. Sometimes our gifts and calling manifest themselves and we are totally unaware of what is going on. Sometimes it causes us to miss our purpose.

Peter simply decides within himself to go fishing. It doesn't say he went out because they were hungry; doesn't say they just needed a few fish to fry. If that was the case, if all they needed was a meal, he probably could have thrown a net from the shore and caught enough fish.

Perhaps he thought, ministry wise, he was finished. After all, Jesus was no longer with them. He had appeared to them after the resurrection, but I think Peter was a little lost and restless and didn't know what to do or where to go. So, he was simply doing what he knew how to do. He was leaning on his own understanding. Proverbs 3:5 says,
"Trust in the Lord with all thine heart; and lean not unto thine own understanding."

When you try to send yourself, when you decide in your own self what you should be doing, your trip will be extremely unfruitful. Verse 3 says they fished ALL night and caught NOTHING! Pretty sure Peter hadn't prayed for direction. He just moved and took the others with him. Now they are all tired, hungry, and empty.

Don't you love it when you have nothing left to give and Jesus is waiting for you on the shore? There he is, appearing to them again, coming to rescue them from their mess. First, he asks if they have any fish? He knows the answer, but you know we need to admit our faults and our failures before help can be accepted. We have to admit we tried to do something, and it didn't work out the way we were expecting. When we can admit our shortcomings, then and only then can Jesus truly work in our lives. Otherwise, we will just keep trusting in ourselves. We will keep walking and moving in our own thinking. We will keep getting the same results time and time again.

When they admitted they didn't have any fish, Jesus commanded them to cast their net one more time. Cast it on the right side, he said. At this point, they have another decision to make. They could listen to the person on the shore or they could choose to pass. Remember they are tired, hungry and they don't know it's Jesus talking to them.

I am pretty sure they're looking over the edge of the boat at this point. They don't see any fish and yet they choose to cast their net anyways. When they do...the net is so full they can't pull it in. When Jesus directs your path and you do exactly what he says to do, your results will be fruitful. Whether it is one soul, a boat load of fish, paying for someone's meal, taking a meal to someone who has recently had surgery or visiting someone in the hospital. Whatever it is God says to do, it will always bring results.

You can't out give God. You can never out do God. His response to your obedience and unselfishness will always yield a greater return than you could ever expect. He will overwhelm you with his goodness and blessings every time.

QUESTIONS

1. It's important to know who we're following and why. Have you ever just followed? Where did you go? How did you feel when you got there and found out why you were there?

2. Have you ever paid-it-forward or done a random act of kindness? Did you see the outcome? Or did you do it anonymously? These acts are definitely fruitful. What did you do? How did it make you feel and how did your kindness affect the other person(s)?

3. Ever had a grand idea? Something you just knew God wanted you to do; but it didn't seem to work out? Did you pray about it first? Did you ask God? Did he answer you? Or did you just go because you thought that was what you were supposed to do? Write down your experience.

4. On the other hand, have you ever been praying about something and everything just worked together? It was like working on a puzzle and the pieces just snap in, one right after the other. Did you see God working things out for you? What was that experience like?

5. What have you learned from both of these experiences? What are your insights? What did you learn?

MOVING

John 14:3
"And if I go and prepare a place for you, I will come again, and receive you unto myself; that where I am, there ye may be also."

Jesus has promised us if we believe on him here, we will have a place in heaven. One day I am going there. I personally don't care if he has prepared me a room, a cabin or a great big house. There will be no night so I don't think we will be sleeping (I could be wrong). I just want to be there when he calls me home.

THINK ON THIS...
Have you ever had to move? I mean from one house to another, one town to the next or even to a completely different state? It is quite the process. It takes a significant amount of time to get everything in order, cleaned up, packed and cleared out.

When I moved from Florida to Pennsylvania my dad found me an apartment. He paid the deposit and the first month's rent and furnished it for me. I want you to see the big picture here. He prepared a place for me. That's exactly what Jesus said he would do in our scripture verse.

Even though a new place has been prepared, there's still a lot of work to be done before you move in. One of the first things you do before moving is weed out and get rid of stuff. You get rid of all those things that are broken, useless, things you have outgrown or just don't use anymore. Whether you are moving from one place to another or from earth to heaven, you'll still need to get your things in order. No sin will enter into heaven, so it has to be removed and eliminated from your life; before your mansion becomes available.

Revelation 21:27

"Nothing impure will ever enter it (heaven), nor will anyone who does what is shameful or deceitful, but only those whose names are written in the Lamb's book of life. No sin will enter into heaven."

There are some items you'll eliminate because they are old or out of date. Items that have served their purpose but need to be upgraded or replaced. Items like that little end table with a broken leg. It has served its purpose, but you currently have a brick under the broken leg to keep it from tipping over. It might be something bigger like a couch or chair. Spiritually we need to let go of the furniture we have set on, our principles, attitudes, thoughts, morals, etc. to make room for godly attributes. Have you ever had a rose bush? Once a rose blooms it has a short life span. Then you prune the bush to make room for new growth.

In your physical home there are items that are personal and filled with memories. Items you will move and take with you no matter how far you go. The same is true spiritually. Not everything within you needs to be changed, removed or replaced to make heaven. After all, God created you. He formed you in your mother's womb and he placed certain gifts and talents within you for His glory. So, if you are a singer, you'll change the song you sing but the talent will remain. If you're an artist, you'll continue to use your artistic talent but instead of nudes you'll be designing sets or painting scenes that point to God.

If you have chosen to follow Jesus, then he has promised to prepare a place for you. Make every effort to prepare your house for moving day; because the place you are going to is greater than any place you could ever imagine!

QUESTIONS

1. Have you ever had to move? Did you enjoy the process?

2. Have you started to prepare for your move to heaven?
   What have you gotten rid of or replaced? i.e. language,
   attitudes?

3. What are you keeping? i.e. your gifts and talents.

4. Moving generally means moving away from friends.
   There are always a few you stay in touch with no matter
   where we are. Have you made a new circle of friends?
   Who are your friends?

5. Are you finding it difficult to part with stuff? What are
   you having a hard time getting rid of? Habits, friends,
   attitudes, hangouts. Why do you think you are having a
   rough time?

OIL LEVEL

Ephesians 4:31-32
*"Let all bitterness, and wrath, and anger, and clamour,
and evil speaking, be put away from you, with all
malice: And be ye kind one to another, tenderhearted,
forgiving one another, even as God for Christ's sake
hath forgiven you."*

Paul is reminding the church in Ephesus of how the new
creature acts, walks, talks and treats people. The old man is
dead. A new man is left in his place once you have accepted
Jesus as your Lord and Savior.

THINK ON THIS
I heard the Lord clearly speak to me one night as I lay down
to go to sleep. He said, "Don't let your oil leak out." I
pondered his word for a couple of days, asking him
questions and answering myself back. "What do you mean
'leak out'?"

So, I asked if he was talking about slacking off in reading
the word, praying, fasting, fellowshipping and my next
thought was, no; those things add oil. I was looking for
what would cause a leak in someone's vessel. I was looking
for a leaky valve or seal. Something rather inconspicuous.
An issue we wouldn't notice until we realized our oil level
was low.

I was starting to understand when I heard a woman testify
one morning. She had no idea God was using her to clue
me in; but when she spoke a little light went on in my head.
She was talking about the little foxes that spoil the vine.
She said, "Don't worry about it if someone thinks your dress
is ugly. If they don't like it, they can go buy you a new
dress. It's your dress and you can wear it if you want to."

All of a sudden, I understood our vessels get cracked when
we indulge ourselves in anger, unforgiveness, bitterness,

envy, jealousy, all those things we read about in our scripture verse today. These emotions cause tiny cracks, small oil leaks, in our vessel. They are little foxes that seem innocuous. A small pity party here, an indignant thought there and the crack begins to form. Unless we rein in our emotions, unless we discuss how we feel and get those emotions resolved, the little crack lengthens and wears away allowing more and more of our oil to pour out.

Have you ever had a leak in your radiator? Allowing a tiny crack in your vessel is just like that. You don't realize anything is wrong until your car overheats. Here's the other problem with a leak. If you don't forgive, if you let hurt or anger fester, that tiny crack will eventually spread. Soon your little leak is a steady drip, which turns into a running stream before turning into a full-on deluge.

You may be doing those things we said adds oil like praying, reading, fasting, fellowshipping. If you have ever had a car that burns oil you know it always starts out with a little drip. You begin by adding a little oil here and a little oil there. Soon it needs a whole quart every week until you are at the point of every time you start the car it needs oil just to crank. Sometimes you can be going through all the motions of reading, praying and church; yet your anger, hatred and, unforgiveness is draining oil faster than you are putting in.

When we get to the point where our oil is leaking out faster than we are putting it in, we are already backsliding. Our walk is a little different then our cars. Our cars should hold the oil and only need to be replaced about every 5,000 miles. Our vessels need oil added daily; it keeps us walking and talking. The less oil we add the deeper the cracks. When our oil levels are extremely low, we are in grave danger of our light going out.

QUESTIONS

1. If you are honest with yourself, are you leaking oil?
   What's causing your leak?

2. How are you dealing with the leak? Are you stuffing your
   feelings; pretending they don't exist? Or are you spewing
   your emotions like a volcano? Do you know they both
   create cracks that lead to leaks?

3. Are you familiar with the scripture that says, "Take us the
   foxes, the little foxes that spoil the vines: for our vines
   have tender grapes." It's from Song of Solomon 2:15. The
   little foxes refer to the small things we tend to overlook;
   but those are the very things stealing the blossoms off
   our vines. It takes blossoms to grow fruit. The little
   foxes are those emotions which cause the leaks. How are
   you going to handle the little foxes? How are you going
   to keep them from eating more blossoms off your vine?

4. Are you adding oil daily? It seems people tend to carry their bible to church, take it home, and set it down until next Sunday. Where is your bible during the week? Are you reading it, studying it, are you hiding the word in your heart?

5. What verse comes to mind when you feel overwhelmed or hurt?

What's in Your Hands

Nehemiah 4:16-18

"From that day on, half of my men did the work, while the other half were equipped with spears, shields, bows and armor. The officers posted themselves behind all the people of Judah who were building the wall. Those who carried materials did their work with one hand and held a weapon in the other, and each of the builders wore his sword at his side as he worked. But the man who sounded the trumpet stayed with me."

Nehemiah and his men were trying to repair the walls of their town. Wherever good is being done, there will always be someone speaking evil and trying to dissuade you from your work.

THINK ON THIS...

We need to be like the workers in this passage from Nehemiah. It says, "Each of the builders wore his sword at his side as he worked." We need to be like these workers. We need to be working for God on one hand, yet ready with our sword on the other.

When we meet a person, who is hurting and in need of a savior, we need to work the ground. Sometimes we need to plow up the fallow ground. People grow hard and dry, their lives become full of rocks, stones and pebbles that need to be turned up and moved out of the way. If you have ever planted a garden you know what I am talking about. You can't plant seed on top of parched ground. You can't plant and expect things to grow up and around large rocks and stones. You need to move the obstacles out of the way for good healthy plants.

Sometimes you need to get down on your knees to weed. You need to grab your little clippers to prune what's dead or overgrown making room for new growth. People tend to listen to everything they hear or read. They accumulate ideas about what it means to worship or ideas about what it means to be a Christian. Most of these ideas shoot up as weeds and choke out the true word and doctrine of the gospel. Weeding needs to be done delicately or you'll pull out the good with the bad. I wouldn't want to pull up my tomato plant when I pull up the dandelions.

On the other hand, we need to carry our sword for when battles ensue. Jesus used the word when he was tempted in the wilderness. He pulled out his sword to fight the spiritual battle. We have to use our sword when the enemy tries to deter us, when the enemy tries to tear down and destroy, we have to know what the word says so we can stand on it. There is power in the word of God. Everything that proceeds out of your mouth has the ability to bless or to curse, it has the ability to bind or to loose.

Whether you are using your bible as a tool or a sword you need to, *"Study to shew thyself approved unto God, a workman that needeth not to be ashamed, rightly dividing the word of truth."* 2 Timothy 2:15
You need to know the word, what it means and stands for. You also need to know when to use it as a tool and when to use it as a sword. Otherwise, the one you wanted to help, you might well destroy.

It is the responsibility of each of us to study the word. You never know who you might be saving. Maybe you say a prayer of faith, knowing, *"the effectual fervent prayer of a righteous man availeth much"* or that the person *"shall live and not die and declare the works of the Lord"*. You have to know the verse that says, *"By his stripes you are healed"* in order to put it to work. Strap on your sword, carry it, read it and use it to your best advantage in every situation of your life.

QUESTIONS

1. What is your favorite scripture verse? Write it down with chapter and verse.

2. Can you use this verse as a tool, a sword or both? Give an example of a situation where you could use this verse and whether it is a tool or a sword. Example: James 3:5, "Even so the tongue is a little member, and boasteth great things. Behold, how great a matter a little fire kindleth!" I am using it as a tool to teach the importance of the words we speak.

3. Think about the tools in your toolbox or shed. Do you own tools that could also be used as a weapon? Weapons that could be used as a tool? Objects, like the word, can often be used for more than one purpose.

4. As a Christian, we need to be on our guard. We should constantly be working on our building, on our walk with Jesus. While at the same time ready to pray, ready to listen, ready to share the word, ready to stand in the gap. Do you have the word hidden in your heart? Can you talk about it? Even if you can't quote chapter and verse do you know what it says?

5. Has the word ever protected you or your family? What was the situation and how did the word work?

PENALTY PHASE

DEUTERONOMY 31:1-2

*"And Moses went and spake these words unto all Israel.
And he said unto them, I am an hundred and twenty
years old this day; I can no more go out and come in:
also the Lord hath said unto me, Thou shalt not go
over this Jordan."*

Twice the people complained to Moses that there was no
water to drink. The first time in Exodus 17 where the Lord
instructed him to take the elders and his staff and go to Mt
Horeb where the Lord would stand before him and he was to
strike the rock one time and water would issue forward. The
second time was Numbers 20, but the instructions were
different this time. Moses was to take his rod with him, he
and Aaron were told to speak to the rock; then the water
would rush forth in front of their eyes. Moses was so angry
at the people though that he struck the rock twice instead.

THINK ON THIS...

Because Moses was disobedient, striking the rock instead of
speaking to the rock, he was penalized by God. He would
never step foot in the promised land. A land he has desired
to see. A land he has been leading these ungrateful,
murmuring people towards. A land for which, he has stood
in the gap and prayed numerous times asking God to spare
these people that they might receive the promise. And now,
Moses is denied entry.

At first glance that seems a mighty heavy penalty. After all,
he simply struck a rock two times instead of speaking to it.
Who wouldn't be perturbed and a tad bit angry dealing with
all those whiny, pouting people? But when you understand
the importance of that single rock, in that single moment of
time, everything changes. The rock was a representation of
Christ and Moses just ruined the entire visual God was
creating. It changes the depth of Moses' disobedience.

It doesn't tell how old Moses was when he struck the rock twice. Nor does it tell how many years passed between that incident and this moment; when he is allowed his first glimpse of the land. I am sure several years, if not a decade or more has passed. It doesn't change the fact that God charged Moses with a penalty; or that the penalty hasn't changed. This is where the consequence for Moses' action is paid.

It struck me how parents today could benefit from this one small passage. In this day and hour when discipline and child rearing no longer go hand-in-hand. Spanking is detrimental to your child's IQ they claim. We see more and more Grandparents trying to raise their children's children and they simply do not have the strength or tenacity at this junction of their life to keep up with them. To parents who simply feel children ought to raise themselves. To everyone gets a trophy because no child should be left out or feel unaccomplished. We have forgotten the need for consequences. Consequences develop character, create boundaries, they strengthen moral fibers. Yet there are few consequences meted out today and even where they are given there is very little follow up. Consequentially, few penalties are ever bestowed.

Children whine or throw tantrums and parents simply do not want to hear it. So, the devices i.e. video games, phones, laptops, etc which are confiscated at first are soon given back and in fact no penalty is paid for the child's bad behavior. It's like giving a convict 10 years for stealing and paroling them after only 1 year. It is gravely important parents follow through on the penalty phase with their children. If I don't follow through on the penalty phase at age 2 for throwing a tantrum and I don't follow through at age 5 for throwing a tantrum and I don't follow through at age 8 or 10 or 12 then what?   At what age do I begin to sincerely hold my child responsible for their behavior? How do I teach them there are consequences for their actions?

Ultimately, who is responsible when the behavior of these teenagers or young adults land in jail? It is the child who will suffer the penalty but who is responsible for the behavior they are asserting? Why shouldn't they believe they can throw a tantrum in front of a judge and go home? Unfortunately, some young people lose their lives because they fail to understand there are consequences for their actions.

The bible says, *"He that spareth his rod hateth his son: but he that loveth him chasteneth him betimes."*
Proverbs 13:24

Discipline is a form of love. Shaping a child's behavior, teaching them right from wrong, teaching them respect, and providing them with boundaries are necessities every parent should afford their children.

QUESTIONS

1. How does your parenting differ from the way your parents parented you? For example: did you have curfews, were you ever spanked, placed in time out, did you have chores, etc. Compare and contrast your parenting to your parents.

2. Do you think discipline is a necessity? Make your argument here for or against.

3. If you had been Moses, could you have continued to lead the people after God penalized you so heavily for striking the rock twice? How do you think it would have affected you?

4. Do you think discipline is needed in the church? Why or why not? If yes, in what areas of the church do you think discipline is needed?

5. What about discipline in government? What changes would you make? What consequences would you levy? How would you get those elected back to working for the people?

RECOVER

2 TIMOTHY 2:26
"And that they may recover themselves out of the snare of the devil, who are taken captive by him at his will."

Paul has been describing how a person can repent and work to make themselves a useable vessel and telling Timothy how to approach people in meekness, sharing the knowledge of Jesus in the hope that someone would repent.

THINK ON THIS...
Here is another way the enemy confuses people. Sinners think they are choosing what they do, when they do it and with whom they do it. They think they are fully in control of their lives. So naturally, it only stands to reason, if they should repent then God would hard wire them so they would do his will and his bidding. Hence, they would be God's slaves.

Paul completely contradicts that. He says repentance would save them from the devil's snare. It would keep them from being his captive and doing his will. What do you think about that?

Have you ever read any of Frank Peretti's books? He had a couple of books called "This Present Darkness" and "Piercing the Darkness" but he has written any number of books including some for teens. In these two books though, he would describe the demons as having long talons and they would dig these talons into people's minds. There by taking control of their thoughts, actions and words. It has been probably 15 or so years since I read those books, but that imagery has always stuck with me.

The devil plays with people like they are puppets. People think they are having fun, but if it is so much fun, how come it causes so much pain and regret? Even in the midst of what they are doing they have pain. The pain isn't a side effect after repenting; though it does hurt badly. It hurts when you think of all the stupid stuff you have done. It hurts when you realize how badly it must have hurt Jesus. He died for our sins, yet he had to watch us day in and day out as we carried on in our mess. He loved us the whole time we were running, digging our hole deeper and wider.

If we could only make people understand liberty comes with repentance. True freedom, true choice comes with choosing Jesus. Now, I choose to leave those things behind me that cause me pain. I can still love on those I once hung out with, but I don't have to hang with them in all the same places. I can be secure in the knowledge I am loved beyond measure. Isn't that what most people are looking for anyway? Looking in all the wrong places and faces.

QUESTIONS

1. How does it make you feel to think the enemy was pulling your strings and you chose to just go along?

2. Did you realize the enemy sets traps trying to ensnare you? If we aren't careful, we can find ourselves in a place or situation that is extremely detrimental. You have to understand the enemy knows your past. Therefore, he knows your weaknesses and he will use them to his advantage.

3. Have you ever had a moment when you realized how much you must have grieved God? Can you describe those feeling?

4. Since you repented, have you experienced freedom? Did you feel the weight of sin lift off of you?

5. Some believe there are too many rules when you are a Christian. What do you say to that?

SING ANYWAY

Psalm 137:3
"For there they that carried us away captive required of us a song; and they that wasted us required of us mirth, saying, Sing us one of the songs of Zion."

Israel has been carried away, taken captive and in the psalm, it says they have hung their harps in the trees. They have given up. While their captors taunt them to sing their songs.

THINK ON THIS...
Paul and Silas were deep into the dark, damp prison. Held for their beliefs, held for preaching the gospel and late at night they began to sing. They praised God, worshipped him in the middle of their circumstances. They knew where their hope lied. Not only did they sing to God for themselves, but everyone within the prison walls heard their songs of praise as well.

What do you do in your midnight hour when everything seems impossible? Do you sing? Do you pray? Or do you fall into despair? Do you know God is going to make a way? Do you know everything is going to be ok and God's got you? Or do you ask him where he is and why he has left you?

The Israelites have hung their harps in the trees. They have abandoned their praise and refused to sing. I'm sure the Babylonians didn't really want to hear their songs. They were just taunting them. Just picking at their open wounds if you will. They should have picked up their harps. Sing anyways! They should have sung their praises to the God who saves. Should have sung their songs that recounted how God saved them in the past. Because who knows....God could have shown up right there and then for them; just like he did for Paul and Silas.

It isn't always easy to sing. Not when you are hurting deeply, not when you are grieving, not when life is spinning out of control but if there is a shimmer of hope inside...sing anyway. The bibles says, *"Put on the garment of praise for the spirit of heaviness."* (Isaiah 61:3)
There is something about singing that calms us.

I encourage you today to sing anyway. No matter what trial you are facing. No matter how bad your situation seems. Sing anyway and see what God will do for you.

<u>QUESTIONS</u>

1. Do you have a favorite song to sing when you are having a hard day? What's the name of it?

2. What is it about that song that picks you up? That gives you hope?

3. After you have sung it a time or two, or three or four, does it make you feel like you can keep going? Does it make you want to sing something else? Does it make you want to shout?

4. Singing soothes; David would play skillfully upon his harp when the evil spirit tormented Saul. Only David's music would calm Saul. When has music calmed you or someone else?

5. "Put on the garment of praise for the spirit of heaviness." (Isaiah 61:3) Only praise swiftly lifts a persons spirit. It seems to vibrate within our being. It touches are emotions. A song can strengthen us, or it can tear us apart. Sad songs drain us. Energetic songs pump us. What song sweeps you away emotionally? Maybe it was a song you played when you were angry or after a bad breakup or it reminds you of a special moment. It's important we understand how music shifts our moods and emotions.

TAKEN CARE OF

2 SAMUEL 8:6
"Then David put garrisons in Syria of Damascus: and the Syrians became servants to David, and brought gifts. And the Lord preserved David whithersoever he went."

David is out fighting the battles, but no matter where he goes, God watches over him and takes care of him. God prospers him, makes him victorious and receives the glory for it.

THINK ON THIS...
"And the Lord preserved David whithersoever he went." WOW! Can you imagine knowing no matter what battle you were in, no matter how big the giants you faced, no matter how strong the enemy or how many troops there were coming against you, God himself would preserve you? David must have been extra special in the sight of God; don't you think?

David was a man after God's own heart. The word declares it to be so in I Samuel 13:14. However, in Romans 2:11 it declares, *"For there is no respect of persons with God."* God did not do something for David that he will not do for you and me. We just need to be like David; desiring and working to have a heart after God.

I can testify, in our years of being full-time on the road, God has preserved us. We have only broken down one time on the road. One time, when we weren't at a church or sitting in someone's yard, where we had help right at our fingertips. That one time though, God kept the tow truck busy so he couldn't get to us, which kept us from being towed to a garage that would have charged us an exorbitant amount for labor. Instead, 2 days later, a friend drove over 100 miles to come to our rescue. He found it was our water pump and the whole thing cost less than $50! Oh, because the tow truck didn't come when it was supposed to...we received a year's free roadside assistance. God can preserve you and see that you get gifts! Just like David received.

We aren't special or better than anyone else, but I can definitely see where God has watched over us. He has kept us when the brakes were basically non-existent, when the breather tube on the gas line was cut, when the gearbox went out and the hot water heater rusted through. Twice we had wires burn up the length of the bus and burn themselves out damaging NOTHING!! God will preserve you; if you seek and desire to be like him.

Do you have a heart after God's own heart? If so, he is preserving you. Think back over the times when circumstances could have been a lot different. Remember exactly how God worked in your life and give him praise for it. It is good to revisit those moments in your life and praise him a second, third, fourth time even. God likes to know that you remember his goodness towards you.

If your heart is hard, if it is stubborn, partial, etc. pray for God to help you. Pray for him to show you how to be more like him in his love for people. After all, God wants to give you his very best.

QUESTIONS

1. Can you testify of a time when God watched over you? When he kept you safe from harm? Write it down

2. Have bad circumstances ever worked out for your good? Like when we received the free roadside assistance for a year. It was actually better for us the tow truck never arrived and then we were blessed on top of it. What is your story?

3. Has God ever sent a friend by your way? Someone who helped you in a time of trouble. A true godsend. Maybe their help saved you a lot of money or allowed you to get to work on time. Maybe they kept your child so you could get to the hospital or just to give you a break to clear your head. Who did he send and what did they do?

4. Has a complete stranger ever helped you? Maybe you were broken down along the road or having a bad day and they smiled and spoke to see if you were ok. Maybe they paid for your meal or groceries. How did a complete stranger help you?

5. Have you ever felt like God sent a sign just for you? In the middle of a bad day or situation, something out of the usual happened and you just knew it was God. What did he do just for you? How did he show his love for you?

TIME

ECCLESIASTES 3:1

"To everything there is a season, and a time to every purpose under the heaven."

Solomon realized that everything in life happens in its own season and each season comes to every person who lives. It doesn't matter what generation you were born in, regardless of the century or era, regardless of whether you believe in God or not, regardless of ethnic origin, country, social status, and on down the line, if you live you will go through the seasons of life.

THINK ON THIS...

Time stops for no man. It doesn't matter what is happening in your life; time keeps marching on. It keeps moving forward. It keeps pressing to the next second, minute, hour nothing stops it. Keep going it says to us; keep walking.

Now I know in Joshua 10:13 the sun stayed in place while they pursued their enemies. It reports it stayed for about a whole day. God made a special provision and I believe it happened with my whole heart. Just like when Elijah prayed and it didn't rain for 3 ½ years. Then he prayed again and it rained upon the earth. God is in control and he will create miraculous circumstances when needed.

However, Solomon is talking about life events. He says there is a time for everything in your life and in mine. We rejoice over the birth of a new baby and mourn the death of a loved one. New crops are planted every spring and harvested every fall, both those planted by the farmer and those we plant and harvest in our spiritual and physical lives. There are times when new avenues open in our lives and then there are times when we need to prune away and remove people, activities or jobs out of our lives.

We need to be like time. No matter what comes to us, no matter what season we are living in, we need to keep ticking. We need to keep pressing, moving forward and striving to reach the next second, minute and hour. There are events in our lives where we would like time to stop. If time stopped the pain might go away, if time could be rewound, we could have an extra day or even an hour, to say the things we didn't say before it was too late. But time doesn't stop; you can't take it back or undo it.

On the other hand, time has a way of easing pain if we let it. Some people try to hold on to the feelings of an exact moment. If they let that moment go and press forward, they feel guilt at moving on when their loved one's life has ended. Or they are afraid of forgetting every aspect of that person. Time is moving but they are not. Sometimes events happen which cause us to let go of time. We fall into great depressions allowing the ebb and flow of our emotions, which create great swells of void inside of us. When we finally wake up out of it, some unfortunately never wake up, time has moved on and we have missed out on the life that was happening all around us.

Make today count. Redeem the time you have so you don't regret missed opportunities or leave things unsaid. I heard someone say one time, "You are only promised the breath you are breathing. The next is never promised to you." In the breath you are breathing what are you going to do with it?

QUESTIONS

1. Have you ever wanted to just hold on to a certain moment in time? What was the occasion? Write it here.

2. Have you ever gotten stuck in your grief? Not wanting to move or unable to move on? Write down your experience. Are you still stuck or have you learned how to keep going?

3. Having been greatly depressed I know how it feels to lose time. Have you ever lost time? One day you realize life has been passing you by and you don't know where the time went. It's like you were present and yet not actually a part of Life. Have you been there? Tell about your experience.

4. If you could make time stop for a day, only one day, what day would it be? If you could make it stop, do you think it would change the pain or make the memory any clearer? What would it accomplish? Eventually time has to start again.

5. We can't go back; we can only go forward. So, starting today, what will you do different? How are you going to redeem the time you have left? What are you going to do with that breath you are breathing in?

WALK BY FAITH

2 Corinthians 5:7
"For we walk by faith, not by sight"

Paul was encouraging the Corinthian church. We all need to be encouraged on occasion. We also need to be instructed, helped and assisted.

THINK ON THIS...
Sometimes, walking by faith is like driving through a bad storm. When the rain is torrential and the skies are dark, you can't depend on following the person in front of you. Have you ever tried to do that? I did once in a bad snowstorm on a major highway. Whew!! All I could see were tiny red beams of light in the whiteout.

Their taillights are barely visible and sometimes they completely disappear out of sight. What if the person you're following veers off the road themselves or turns onto a different road; taking you way off course? We can't depend on someone else to lead us through our storm.

Sometimes the storm is so fierce, the best course of action is too pull off and wait it out. Moses told the people to stand still and see the salvation of the Lord in Exodus 14. The Egyptians were hot on their trail and the Red Sea was laid out in front of them. All they could do was camp out and wait for the storm to pass. In their case, wait for God to part the waters and create dry ground. There are times in our lives when circumstances seem to be swirling all around us and one wrong move could jeopardize everything. Those are the moments where we need to stand still and wait.

It's dangerous to plow full steam ahead when your path is obscured from the storm. You could get stalled out driving through deep water and stranded. You could also run over debris in the road; causing you to lose control of your vehicle, blow out a tire or cause an accident involving others.

While the rain is beneficial to our well-being it can also be a dangerous and even a deadly adversary. We need to be aware of our surroundings, aware of the storm and the direction in which it is heading. Paying a little attention to the details could save you a lot of trouble in the end. You might choose a different route, change your timing, or even change your plans all together.

In the end, storms bring about growth and new fruit in our spiritual life just as the rain brings about growth and life all around us. Storms create ambivalent emotions to rise up inside of us. On one hand we want to grow in the Lord, we want to bear fruit and become everything he created us to be. On the other hand, we like to be comfortable. Storms bring stress, discomfort, change, they make us slow down and wait. Sometimes they sideline us. We are left sitting on the edge of the road; until they pass or slow down and we can see the white lines again. Storms change the atmosphere. Once they pass, they can either bring the temperature down several degrees or it can change into pure humidity, making it feel several degrees hotter than the actual temperature outside. The same holds true in our spiritual lives as well.

Next time you find yourself in a storm, remember it is better to slow down than to go full speed ahead. Let God part the waters and dry the ground so you can safely pass through.

QUESTIONS

1. Have you ever been in a physical storm where you couldn't see the road very clearly? What did you do? Did you plow full steam ahead taking chances or did you pull of the road or under an overpass to wait it out?

2. When it's out of your control how do you respond? Do you become frantic? Anxious? Calm? Do you take charge or follow? Describe a moment when it was out of your control, what happened, what did you do & how did it turn out.

3. Do you handle spiritual storms the same way? Those storms, where all you can do is pray. Do you beg and plead with God? Do you thank him before you see the answer? Are you reminded of bible stories where God came through? Do you recall other storms you have weathered? Or do you sit in a ball and fall apart just waiting for someone to take care of you?

4. Testify. Write down a storm you made it through when prayer was your only defense. Be honest, if you fell apart say so. Sometimes we can fall apart in one moment and praise God for his blessings the next. In Psalms you can find David falling apart, crying and pleading at the beginning but by the end he was remembering what God had done before. He was reassured God would do it again. Eventually, he would praise God, confessing this time was no different as he thanked God for his blessings.

5. Do you have a favorite scripture when storms come? If not find one. Write it down.

WHICH ONE

EXODUS 15:24

"And the people murmured against Moses, saying, What shall we drink?"

"So Moses brought Israel from the Red Sea, and they went out into the wilderness of Shur; and they went **three days** in the wilderness, and found no water. And when they came to Marah, they could not drink of the waters of Marah, for they were bitter"

THINK ON THIS...

Can you imagine if three days ago several million of us were escaping for our lives? Our enemy is practically breathing down our necks and we come to the Mississippi River; where we find no way to escape our pending doom. We think all hope is lost when suddenly this large cloud stands between them and us. It gives off light on our side and total darkness on their side. A strong wind begins to blow across the river, we watch as the waters part, cutting a large swath through the middle. After several hours we walk on a dry riverbed safely crossing to the other side. Then we watch as our enemy tries to make their way across, the wind stops blowing and the waters crash over them; killing every last person.

For how long do you think that memory would sustain you? Would you think that Moses was responsible for bringing you through the river? Would you credit Moses for drowning every troop of the enemy? Would you think Moses pulled off each of the plagues that occurred in Egypt? Who would you be looking to Moses as your savior and guide?

Don't be too quick to judge the Israelites. We do the same thing today when it comes to our pastor. We start looking to our pastor as the source of our miracle. It's because he prayed or because of what he said or he did and we give him all the credit, we give all of God's glory away. We also forget the last blessing when the next circumstance or trial comes around. Isn't that what has happened here in our verse for today? Three days earlier God brought them safely across the Red Sea and obliterated their enemy. As a matter of fact, God has been constantly with them night and day. He has been a visible pillar of cloud by day and a pillar of fire in the night. But now they are thirsty.

They are thirsty, they are walking, they are probably hot and dirty. Did I mention they are thirsty? God is right there before them, but they murmur about Moses and expect Moses to meet their need. They forget Moses is just a man. He is just like them. He is a human being, born of a woman, born in sin, walking in faith, hot, tired and thirsty just like all of them. Yet, they expect him to give millions of them water to drink.

It seems Moses is the only one bringing the petition for water to the Lord. Millions of people who all have the same need and only one goes to the true source. Only Moses goes to one who can create rivers in the middle of the desert. In the modern-day church, we want revival and miracles and provision, but we all look to the pastor as if he is the only one who can pray, seek and reach God.

I just wanted to remind you today to keep your eyes upon Jesus. Pray for your pastor and remember he's just a man doing his best to be a good leader and example in the church and community where he lives.

QUESTIONS

1. Have you ever put your pastor up on a pedestal? Why did you elevate him so?

2. Have you had a pastor who fell? How did you feel about him afterwards?

3. Do you expect your pastor to do all the work? To visit the sick, to pray, to fast, to manage all of the maintenance and upkeep at the church? In smaller churches, the pastor is often working a full-time job to support his family on top of everything the church requires. What is it you expect of your pastor?

4. Millions of people were traveling with Moses, but it never says they prayed. It never says they did anything but murmur and complain. Do you tend to murmur and complain like the Israelites? Do you ask the pastor to pray but fail to pray for yourself?

5. We can simply be a part of the congregation or we can be an integral part of the church. We can be workers, doers, pray warriors, visitors of the sick, shut-ins, greeters, etc. What are you doing? Are you a pew sitter or a church worker? What are you doing?

NEW GARMENT

ZECHARIAH 3:4

"And he answered and spake unto those that stood before him, saying, Take away the filthy garments from him. And unto him he said, Behold, I have caused thine iniquity to pass from thee, and I will clothe thee with change of raiment."

Zechariah is relating the vision he is having. He is watching the angel speak to Joshua the High Priest. The priesthood was defiled, the people were defiled, they were far from God; but once again God was offering to be their God if they would turn and walk towards him once again.

THINK ON THIS...

When we repent, God forgives us. When we are baptized though, our sins are washed away as far as the east is from the west. I don't know if you have ever thought of it this way or not but contemplate it for just a moment.

In Acts 2:38 Peter told the crowd they needed to repent and be baptized for the REMISSION of their sins. Now if a person's sin was removed when they repented what would be the purpose of baptism? Baptism is like a spiritual bath to wash away all the dirt and grime of our past. Once you are washed and clean don't you need a new garment to put on? We need a garment like the angel gave to Joshua in our verse. I have never taken a shower and then reached for the dirty, sweaty clothes I was glad to slip out of.

Sometimes I find people have a hard time forgiving themselves. They know they repented and were forgiven. They were baptized and became a new creature; but they are still beating themselves up. They can't forget or forgive themselves for their past mistakes, for the very things Jesus died for and put under the blood. Those filthy garments are disposed of and forgotten by God. They aren't ours to put on anymore. When you start to feel beat down because of your past, tell the devil you remember that person and PRAISE GOD because that isn't who you are now! Jesus gave you a new garment. He gave you armor. Complete with a helmet of salvation, a belt of truth, a breastplate of righteousness, shoes of peace, a shield of faith and the word for a sword. You are outfitted and ready to go!

Do you remember when you were in school and during those first few days you wore the new clothes your parents bought you? We would put on those new clothes and strut our stuff. It feels good to put on a new outfit. It boosts our morale. It's funny isn't it, how an outfit can make you feel confident, cute, silly, unique, so on and so on?

I hope you will consider the garment you're wearing; spiritually speaking. Is it a filthy rag or is it a spotless garment? Remember it only takes one stain to soil your favorite shirt. Spiritually or physically speaking. Put on your armor and walk in Godly confidence today.

QUESTIONS

1. Do you still beat yourself up over past mistakes, choices, decisions, and friends? Do you wallow in those things or have you learned to move past them?

2. Does remembering those past things have any useful purpose in your life today? Why or why not?

3. We all get stains on our clothing. Stains from food, grease, and dirt. If you get a spot on your spiritual garment how do you clean it? You need to get it out and SHOUT isn't up to the task.

4. Have you been baptized? There is a school of thought that says repentance is the only thing required to make heaven. Some were christened or baptized as a child; they believe they have satisfied that requirement. Do you need to be baptized after you repent and make a confession of your faith? Do you have scripture to back up your belief? What is it?

5. Have you ever noticed how different outfits make you feel about yourself? When we look a mess, we feel like a mess and when we look all put together, we feel that. It works the same way with spiritual garments too. We put on a garment of praise it changes things, we put on a garment of salvation and it changes things. How do these different garments make you feel?

WHERE ARE YOUR ALTARS

EXODUS 17:15
"And Moses built an altar, and called the name of it Jehovahnissi:"
JOSHUA 8:30
"Then Joshua built an altar unto the Lord God of Israel in mount Ebal"
JUDGES 6:24
"Then Gideon built an altar there unto the Lord, and called it jehovahshalom"

In every one of these instances Moses, Joshua and Gideon built an altar to remember what God had done for them.

THINK ON THIS...
We all have moments in our lives when God moves, speaks, heals, delivers, or saves us; but did you build an altar to commemorate the moment? In the Old Testament, they would recount their history pointing out the altar, and once again praising God. It was there they won a battle, it was there God spared their life, it was there God spoke to them, it was there God provided for their needs, so they built an altar to testify and to remember.

Where are the altars built in your life? What causes you to remember God's goodness to you? My bible is marked at certain passages to remind me when I read it again. I can think of a couple scriptures off the top of my head God has used to help me through difficult times.

John 10:18
"No man taketh it from me, but I lay it down of myself. I have power to lay it down, and I have power to take it again. This commandment have I received of my Father."
Somewhere during my depression, I read this verse and I understood the enemy might harass me, might try to intimidate me but he couldn't take my life from me. I could

lay it down and let him walk all over me or I could pick my life up, live it and be his nightmare.

Mark 10:29-30

"And Jesus answered and said, Verily I say unto you, There is no man that hath left house, or brethren, or sisters, or father, or mother, or wife, or children, or lands, for my sake, and the gospel's, But he shall receive an hundredfold now in this time, houses, and brethren, and sisters, and mothers, and children, and lands, with persecutions; and in the world to come eternal life."

I was going through a rough time one week. Thursday night, campmeeting was starting, I was about 200 miles from home, our daughter had recently been in an accident, my nephew was in the hospital and I was being torn apart emotionally. As I prayed, I heard God saying over and over "forsake mother" and I knew this was the verse he was referring to. I held onto it and by Saturday, God had taken care of everything! He relieved all my stress, provided for my daughter and my nephew was improving.

There are other altars represented by pictures. Pictures of repairs done to our bus; showing how God watched over us and protected us from what could have been a life and death circumstance. Pictures of moments he has allowed us to celebrate and be recognized. Pictures of places, baptisms, weddings, awards, etc.

There are altars of memories as well. Memories I recall when I see someone else struggling, memories I recall when I am going through something and I remind myself of other times God has supplied and come through. Just like David, I encourage myself by revisiting those altars and remembering what God has done in the past.

Take some time today and revisit your altars. Give God thanks all over again for the things he has done.

QUESTIONS:

1. Do you know of any place in the United States that could be considered an altar? A place where something significant happened in American history; a place where you can take your children, point to it and recount the story.

2. In the last several years we have seen statues come down. Pieces of our history. Many of them from the height of civil rights era. Statues like General Robert E. Lee, Jefferson Davis, Thomas J. "Stonewall" Jackson to name a few. These were landmarks, altars of moments and people that caused change within our boundaries. Whether they were right or wrong. They are a part of our history. They have even gone so far as to remove moments form the pages of our children's history books. What is your opinion on the removal of these items? Does removing them change history? Good idea to remove them or bad idea?

3. Do you have anything in your home that could be considered an altar? It might be a photo, an heirloom or something else. What do you have? What does it represent?

4. How do you remember the moments when God poured out a blessing on you? Are there any special altars in your spiritual life? How are they marked?

5. Share the story of one of those altars.

NOT THE ANSWER

GENESIS 29:34
*"And she conceived again, and bare a son; and said,
Now this time will my husband be joined unto me,
because I have born him three sons: therefore was
his name called Levi."*

Leah was married to Jacob. A man who had worked for her
father for 7 years in order to marry her younger sister,
Rachel. On the big day, the girl's dad plied Jacob with wine
during the feast and by evening Jacob couldn't tell who he
was giving his vow to under all those veils or who he was
lying next to in his tent. The next morning, he wakes to find
Leah, not his beloved Rachel. Leah receives one week as a
honeymoon period and then Jacob and Rachel are married.
Jacob works another 7 years for the privilege of marrying
Rachel too. Leah was unwanted and unloved.

THINK ON THIS...
Have you ever known someone who thought having a baby
would help his or her marriage? Couples who think a baby
will bring them together, cause them to grow closer, to have
a greater bond? A baby is not the answer for any flailing
marriage.

Leah is the perfect example. In Genesis 29-30 you will find
the birth of all 6 sons and the 2 sons she received from
Zilpah her handmaid, who she gave to Jacob for a wife.
With every child she makes a statement reflecting how she
feels this birth will affect her marriage and the way her
husband will see her. Upon the birth of her 6th son she
declares the following, *"God has endowed me with good
endowment; now my husband will dwell with me, because I
have borne him six sons."*

A marriage is a work of love between two people. Children
are blessings, not pawns. They aren't meant to be used for
gaining favor or to punish the other parent with. Children

are meant to be an extension of the love between two people. They enrich our healthy relationships and we pour into them. We don't expect them to fix, correct and pour into us.

Either someone loves you or they don't. You can't make them, can't force them. Unfortunately, we grow apart sometimes. We each do our own thing and never meet in the middle. Be ok with just God and let God take care of the rest.

Jacob was forced into a marriage with Leah. He had no choice. He was never told of the custom of the older daughter having to be married first. He worked 7 years for Rachel and woke to Leah. Can you blame him for being resentful? Leah had a part in the deception. I don't know where Rachel was that whole day. It doesn't say she was hidden away. It doesn't tell us if she was deceived or if she knew what was going to happen. I can't imagine how she felt having to share her husband with her sister. How it felt to watch her sister have child upon child before she conceived.

A baby does change everything. It puts stress on the healthiest of marriages. Babies interrupt sleep, demand attention, change schedules, change budgets and definitely change the dynamics between a husband and wife. A child becomes the center of your world and in everything you do they become the prime consideration.

A baby is a blessed event and a huge responsibility. There is nothing like the giggle of a baby or the hug of a small child. The picture they draw for your fridge or the unconditional love they give. As a shared responsibility, it bonds a family together and adds to the love of a home.

QUESTIONS

1. Why do we think a baby will be the glue to bind two people together? If we have to entrap someone, like Jacob was here, is there any hope of true love and happiness?

2. Why do we use our children against our spouse or ex-spouse to get our way? Does it actually work? Is there any pleasure actually gained?

3. When we use our children like that, who are we really hurting? If we love our children, we should want them to have a great relationship with the other parent; our feelings for that person aside. Isn't that love?

4. What is your definition of love?

5. Love is patient, love is kind. It does not envy, it does not boast, it is not proud. It does not dishonor others, it is not self-seeking, it is not easily angered, it keeps no record of wrongs. Love does not delight in evil but rejoices with the truth. It always protects, always trusts, always hopes, always perseveres. Love never fails. 1 Corinthians 13:4-7 (NIV) Love means putting the needs of someone else ahead of ourself. Who do you truly love? Whose needs do you place ahead of your own? Forget the he said, she said and allow your children to love both mom and dad so that they can grow to be productive adults.

CLEANING UP

2 KINGS 23:4

"And the king commanded Hilkiah the high priest, and the priests of the second order, and the keepers of the door, to bring forth out of the temple of the Lord all the vessels that were made for Baal, and for the grove, and for all the host of heaven: and he burned them without Jerusalem in the fields of Kidron, and carried the ashes of them unto Beth-el."

Josiah was cleaning house and taking back God's house. He was being a true example to the people. He didn't just order others to do the clean-up. He pitched in. He burned, he stomped, he carried the ashes.

THINK ON THIS...

I wonder what King Josiah would order out of our churches today? Think about where you go to worship the Lord for a moment. Is there anything in the house that represents another god? Are there any practices that don't truly focus on God and his sovereignty? I just want you to think for a moment. We aren't putting anyone down or criticizing. Remember everything in this book it simply to make you think and consider.

There are somethings we do and say, truly believing we are remembering Jesus or celebrating certain events in his life. The truth is however, they don't represent him at all and they came out of pagan practices. Sometimes in our zeal to win souls we offer events that attract people and we end up bringing parts of the world into the church house.

I wonder what Josiah would think about all the flashing lights, smoke machines and other objects we have brought out of the bar and concert scenes to create flash and bang trying to evoke emotions in our congregations? Again, not condemning anybody; I am just wondering.

148

I wonder if Josiah would go along with egg hunts and sunrise services or decorated trees on our platforms. All of their origins are found in pagan worship rituals. Hundreds of years ago, some well-meaning person thought, "Hey, I bet we could entice new people if we hide eggs too. People will bring their children to participate and we can share Jesus with them." People come to participate but how many of them come back for service?

I know we observe traditions and follow the flow but what would King Josiah do today if he walked into our churches? Because if he, as the king, destroyed or demolished something then what does Jesus think of what we are doing today and what would he do?

We have mentioned in a previous lesson about paying musicians who aren't saved. What about coffee bars in the church or people eating and drinking in the sanctuary or children/teens playing on phones and tablets during the message? You can probably think of some other things as well.

Josiah just made me think and I am trying to make you think as well. What is there in our house of prayer, the place where we go to worship Jesus, that has clouded our worship experience? What have we brought in from the world that Josiah would rip out, break up, ground into ashes and carry far away from the church building?

For that fact, what would he tear down in our own lives and stomp to ashes?

QUESTIONS

1. Did you know Easter egg hunts, Sunrise Services and decorating Christmas Trees started out as pagan rituals? (You can research their origins online. This not a debate just a question.)

2. Do you think it matters if we participate in these things? Personally, or at our church? Does it matter to you and your walk what the old testament says about bringing in traditions from other religions? Think about it.....

3. What first drew you to the church you regularly attend?

4. Do you feel your worship experience needs to look and feel like a concert venue? Why or why not?

5. What do we need for an authentic time of worship? Do we need instruments? Do we need a Praise Team? Do we need professional singers and musicians?

6. If Jesus showed up at your church on Sunday morning would he be pleased? Or would he be like Josiah? What things do you think he would change?

LAYERING

2 CORINTHIANS 8:7
"Therefore, as ye abound in every thing, in faith, and utterance, and knowledge, and in all diligence, and in your love to us, see that ye abound in this grace also."

Paul was instructing the Corinthian church. He had set the church up and they were doing well but then people with other doctrines, people who served other gods came and the people swerved and swayed and forgot what Paul had taught them.

THINK ON THIS...

Growing in Christ is a lot like layering your clothes to go outside when the weather is harsh and cold. You can have a great sweater, but that one layer is not going to keep you warm once you step out into the frigid air. It takes a t-shirt or oxford, then your sweater followed by a warm coat. As children, when we wanted to go outside to play in the snow, we were bundled up tight. You put your gloves on, followed by your one-piece snowsuit. Boots were next, a knit cap and your hat was pulled up and tied before a scarf was wrapped around your neck. Staying warm and protected is all in how you layer your clothing.

I was thinking about the word and how God reveals the layers of it as we grow and mature. In Sunday School class children learn about the main bible characters and characteristics of a Christian. Adam & Eve teaches them about disobedience and how there are consequences for your actions. It is only as we grow and mature in God and gain a deeper understanding that he peels back deeper insight for us. We understand the fig leaves only temporarily covered their nakedness; it only hid them from the world's eyes. When it came to the spiritual ramifications though the fig leaves were inadequate. It takes a blood sacrifice to pay for sin, so an animal had to be sacrificed and clothes were fashioned from the animal's hide.

On another layer we learn the order or hierarchy God created. The husband is the head of the family and then the wife and on down the line. God gave Adam the commandment not to touch the fruit. Adam was responsible to God for what happened in the garden. God put Adam in charge. Eve was responsible to Adam her husband. He must have told her not to gather fruit from that particular tree because she told the serpent they weren't to eat it. We all know what happens. The serpent wears her down, Eve picks the fruit and she and Adam eat it. I have always wonder, if one of them had taken responsibility for their actions would God have allowed them to stay in the garden? But as I am writing God reminded me, they couldn't stay. One bite of that fruit was the same as handing the deed back to the enemy. It was a very expensive dinner they ate that night. The layer here is Eve should have obeyed her husband and not picked the fruit but when she did pick it, Adam should have reprimanded his wife. Instead he ate it. He should have admitted to God that he had disobeyed his word. Adam should have repented with his wife by his side. They both should have been remorseful. Instead they played the blame game. We need to own up to our mistakes and failures.

Yet another layer is found in this same story on tithing. I don't know how many trees were actually planted in the garden but to simplify it we will say there were 10. God said not to touch one tree. That one tree was like our tithe. Whether you have a job, or receive a social security, disability or pension check we have it because God has provided it for us. Therefore, the first 10th of our income belongs to God. When we touch that 10 percent we cause ourselves harm. In Malachai 3:8, God clearly speaks about people robbing him by not giving tithes and offerings into the storehouse.

153

To become a fully mature Christian, we need to have layered the word of God in our lives. We need to be mindful that people are in different stages or layers. Just because they call themselves a Christian doesn't mean they have gotten pass that first or second layer.

If we think of it as being in school, we wouldn't expect a 3rd grader to be responsible for 10th grade work. The problem comes when a person has been sitting in church for 20 years and they're still on a 3rd grade level. We must strive to add, to gain to our understanding. It is up to each of us to be ever growing and learning..

QUESTIONS

1. How many years have you been saved? Be honest now, what grade would you consider yourself to be in? Choose from Kindergarten all the way up to PHD. Explain why you have chosen this grade.

2. Have you ever read a scripture and suddenly it takes on a new meaning? Maybe you gained a greater understanding or saw how it pertained to your life. Tell how it changed your viewpoint.

3. Everything we learn in life we learn through layers. You have to know your numbers to learn how to add, to which we add subtraction and on up the line. Think of one of the first bible stories you learned. Write down how you originally saw the story and what else have you learned about that story as you layered on it.

4. Are there any other aspects of life that comes in layers? It's a great question to ponder. Write down whatever comes to your mind.

5. Isaiah 28:10 says, "For precept must be upon precept, precept upon precept, Line upon line, line upon line, Here a little, there a little." Are you familiar with the verse? If not go over to Isaiah and read through it. What do you think it means? Why is it important?

PARDON ME

Luke 7:12-14

"Now when he came nigh to the gate of the city, behold, there was a dead man carried out, the only son of his mother, and she was a widow: and much people of the city was with her. And when the Lord saw her, he had compassion on her, and said unto her, Weep not. And he came and touched the bier: and they that bare him stood still. And he said, Young man, I say unto thee, Arise."

Jesus and the disciples were just coming into town when a funeral procession started to pass by. Jesus was being Jesus; his compassion reached out to her, to comfort her, he also restored her son to her.

THINK ON THIS...

How many times do we see similar scenarios in the bible? Jesus is passing by and he basically says, "Pardon me" and changes the entire trajectory of a person's life. How often do we say, "Pardon me" when we see people who are hurting? How often do we show compassion to complete strangers? How often do we show compassion to friends and family?

Elijah had a different type of "Pardon me" moment when he went up against the prophets of Baal on Mt. Carmel. He mocked those men, goading them on as they called upon their gods. For hours they chanted and cut themselves trying to get fire to fall from heaven and consume the sacrifice. When Elijah could take no more of their foolishness he screamed, "PARDON ME". It was Elijah's turn to rebuild the altar they had broken down in their chaos and shenanigans. Elijah's turn to call upon the one true God. To prove that his God was the ONLY God. To prove his God had ears to hear and power to answer. Which, as we all know, he did answer and answered above and beyond what the false prophets had even hoped their god would do.

We need to be bold like Elijah and say, "Pardon me" when people are running down our God. When people are using his name in vain. When people are blaming God for their mistakes and failures. When they blame God for illness and devastation. Our God gives good and perfect gifts, James 1:17; anything else is either one's own making or from the enemy of our soul.

David sent his men to Nabal. A wealthy rancher, whose shepherds had tended his flocks near David and his men and David and his men watched out for them. Now though, David and his men need some help. They had never asked for anything before, never required anything from the shepherds for their assistance; they were just being good neighbors. So, David sent his men to ask Nabal for food. They were hungry and it was in a season of plenty for Nabal as they were shearing the sheep. The men said, "Pardon me" and Nabal refused them. David was about to unleash his fury upon Nabal and every male on the ranch. But David was about to encounter Nabal's wife Abigail, who heard what her husband had done and understood the possible consequences of her husband's actions. Quickly, she loaded down the mules and went to head off David. In her "Pardon me" moment, she spoke words of wisdom to David. She spoke of who David was and why Nabal was not worth his effort or the smear on his name. Abigail saved her entire household that day and unbeknownst to her changed her entire future.

Sometimes we need to step in and take care of a mess we didn't make. We need to say "Pardon me" and get to work. We don't need to lay blame, don't need to make a big deal of what we do or how we did it. God sees it and he will reward it in due time.

There are lots of ways to create a "Pardon me" moment. Look for your opportunity to say "Pardon me" this week, this month, this year, this lifetime...

There is someone that is hurting, someone who doesn't know the power of your God, there is probably a mess someplace that needs someone willing to step in and straighten it out; don't be afraid to be the one who speaks, "Pardon me".

QUESTIONS

1. Do you have a "Pardon me" story? A time when you saw a problem and stepped in to pray or handle a situation? What did you do?

2. Have you ever had a time when you should have said "Pardon me" and didn't do it? How did you feel about it later?

3. Has anyone ever said "Pardon me" to you? Has anyone stepped in when you were in distress or really needed a friend? What happened?

4. Pick one of the people I spoke about, the mother (Luke 7:11-17), Elijah (1 Kings 18:1-40) or Abigail (1 Samuel 2-25) and write down how their story would have ended had no one said "Pardon me".

5. Have you ever had a moment when you felt like God was saying "Pardon me"? In the midst of a struggle, valley, wilderness...did you feel like your eyes were suddenly opened to understand or did you get an "AHA" moment where everything became clear? Write it down

PRESS IN

Luke 19:3
"And he sought to see Jesus who he was; and could not for the press, because he was little of stature."

Zaccheus was a short little man. He heard Jesus was going to be passing by, but the crowd was thick, there would be no way to see around all the people. So Zaccheus climbed a tree.

THINK ON THIS...
Imagine standing on the top of a hill and Jesus is on the street below passing by. The hill is filled with people, shoulder to shoulder, amassed and virtually impassable. It's a long way down the hill to the street but you need to get there.

Many of those standing in your way have simply heard about this one called Jesus. They heard he was going to be walking through town, down this road; they just want to catch a glimpse of this man. They want to see who it is everyone is talking about. They don't want anything from him. They don't feel like they need him or need to follow him. They are just spectators. Just taking up space. They are quite simply keeping you from getting to your miracle.

I, however, am on the furthest point up the hill from where Jesus will be passing by on the road. I want to touch him. I want him to touch me. Honestly, I need him to touch me! I have got to do something.

I could choose to stand at the top of the hill and do nothing. I could think there will be another day, another time. I could walk away, the same way I came that day. I could choose to live with the pain in my body, live with the disease that's sapping my strength and energy. I could choose to live in the depression that holds me prisoner. I could choose to do nothing. Or I can choose to be seen. Choose to do whatever it takes to get the attention of Jesus.

So, whether I can push my way through the crowd or not, I am going to make it known that I am there. I'm going to shout, "JESUS!" I'm going to shout, "I NEED YOU! HELP ME! TOUCH ME! JESUS... JESUS... JESUS!" I'm not going to care whose ear I am shouting in. I'm not going to stop no matter how many people shush me or yell to be quiet. I am on a mission.

I know if I can only get his attention my whole world is going to change. Even if I can't push through the crowd, he is able to speak a word that will reach me where I am. I am fully confident and fully persuaded as I push through the crowd, shouting, waving my arms and not caring what anyone else thinks. That some way, somehow, I am going to get his attention. I just need Jesus to hear me. I need Jesus to acknowledge me. A moment is all I need.

A moment in the presence of Jesus is life changing. The woman with the issue of blood pressed through the crowd to touch his garment and was healed. The blind man sitting on the curb called out until Jesus passed by and touched him. Those are just two of the many testimonies it tells in the bible. When people forgot everyone else around them and focused their entire attention on Jesus they were healed and made whole.

QUESTIONS

1. Do you truly believe, I mean believe with all your heart, mind and soul that Jesus still heals like he did in the bible? Not, I believe he will in his time. Or if it's his will. Do you believe when you set all doubt aside God will move for you?

2. Have you ever been healed miraculously or know someone who was? Write that testimony down here.

3. Have you ever had a need when you walked into church and left church with the same need? Maybe you were sick, anxious, needed a financial blessing, needed some peace of mind, were depressed.... Why didn't you go up and ask for prayer?

4. Right now, what do you need? Write it down, no doubts! Tell God you believe it's coming and thank him for it. Every time you think about it simply say I wrote it down Lord, Thank you!

5. Write down 3 scriptures that show God's promise to answer. Scripture where he did it before, scripture that tells of his faithfulness to answer, any scripture that instills confidence in you.
   1.

   2.

   3.

REPEAT

ACTS 19:8

*"And he went into the synagogue, and spake boldly for
the space of three months, disputing and persuading
the things concerning the kingdom of God."*

This is not the first scripture, not the last either, where I find
Paul staying in one place for an extended period of time
expounding Jesus and the written word.

THINK ON THIS...

Do you remember before you were saved? How many times
did someone try to tell you about Jesus? How many times
were you invited to church? How many times did you say
yeah, yeah and disregard everything they were saying to
you? Most people can't count the times.

Have you ever known someone that was in a bad spot and
you shared Jesus? Maybe you took them out to lunch for
the express purpose of sharing and you just knew, today
was the day they were going to cry out and repent; only to
be extremely disappointed? The whole ordeal leaves you
beside yourself. You just can't understand it. How could
they think the life of Jesus was just a nice story? What are
they thinking when they say Christians are just weak and
need a crutch? We tend to end up in an absolute tizzy.

Really??! Our scripture today said Paul was in this place for
three months. He went into great detail explaining how the
old prophesies had been fulfilled. He was trying to convince
people, who already believed in God, to see the truth of
Jesus and their need of him. The Jews, whom Paul is
expounding to, knew the Old Testament inside and out.
They were looking for the Messiah, yet they totally missed
him. Many Christians today don't read the Old Testament.
There are churches that don't preach out of it. However, the
Old Testament is necessary for a complete understanding of

God, who he is and how all those stories and people connect and relate to us.

If you skip to verse 10, you will see Paul was in one place for two years. Skip to verse 18 and he was somewhere else for a year and a half. You know, many of those sitting in the synagogue were the same people day in and day out. Yet, Paul continued to press, he continued to explain with the hope that their spirit would be pricked, praying someone would believe.

Don't be discouraged when you share your faith and the other person doesn't fall to their knees right there and then. Keep sharing the word, share an important point made during the message on Sunday. Testify! No one can take away or discredit what God does for you. Whether or not they recognize him, you recognize him every chance you get.

Remember, it might take a few tries. Shoot, it might take a year, five or twenty but don't stop hoping. Don't stop praying for them. Sometimes we share for years and it seems like we get no response. Then they hear the same message of hope from a different pastor or on TV or from a person at work and suddenly it all makes sense to them. The Spirit draws them, and they respond. You have a part in that soul! God has seen everything you did to reach them. Don't be discouraged. We didn't hear the first time it was presented to us either, but someone kept praying and speaking in our ear.

QUESTIONS

1. Be honest, have you ever gotten discouraged because you witnessed and they rejected what you were saying? Did you think they were just going to "see the light" and give their life to Jesus? Did you give up on them?

2. Are you familiar with 1 Corinthians 3:6? It says, "I have planted, Apollos watered: but God gave the increase."? If you are unfamiliar with it go read chapter 3, pull it up on your phone. What does this scripture mean to you?

3. In the story of The Little Red Hen she wanted to bake a loaf of bread. At every step she asked her friends for help. Help to prepare the ground, to till, to plant seed, to weed, water, harvest, to take the wheat to the mill, and even help to bake it. Seeing a soul saved is a lot like this story. There are a lot of steps. Someone has to break ground, someone plants, someone waters, someone harvests, etc. You'll never know who has worked in a garden (on a soul) before you. But every worker is remembered by God for their labor. Will this change your perspective the next time you witness? What are your thoughts?

4. Think about your own salvation. Make a list here, as complete as you can, of all the people who worked in your garden. How many years did it take from the first worker until you reached the altar?

5. Plants germinate at different rates. In Pennsylvania they say, "corn should be knee high by the fourth of July." Tomatoes, beans, & cucumbers are all ready to pick at various times, but they all have their day. Who is in your garden of souls? These are the people you are praying for. Those you are watering, weeding, etc. Plant seeds by simply interjecting a great point from service during lunch, show kindness or testify. Write down who is in your garden. Who you are praying for and planting seed in?

TRICKERY

Acts 8:10

"To whom they all gave heed from the least to the greatest saying, This man is the great power of God."

Let's back up a verse, because that is where it tells who they think is so great and why they think it. His name is Simon, it plainly states, he used sorcery to bewitch the people and it ends by telling how he boasted to everyone that he was great.

THINK ON THIS...

Simon was tricking people. Maybe he knew some illusions or how to mix a few chemicals together to create a smoke screen or make a loud bang. Thank you for coming today, I am Simon the Great! Pretty soon everyone thinks he's great. He took their money, entertained their eyes and proclaimed he was great. Hook, line and sinker you might say.

When is the last time a true quarterback had to boast how far he could throw a ball? When is the last time Johnny Depp had to boast about his acting skills? How often do you think Pavarotti had to tell someone he had a fantastic tenor voice? Tim Hawkins doesn't have to tell anybody he's funny either. Have you seen any of his YouTube videos? Truthfully, they don't need to boast of their abilities and talents, their abilities and talents speak for themselves. The same is true for great men of God. True prophets don't run around declaring their greatness. Mostly because a true prophet knows he is nothing and it's God who gives the words. Prophets are simply God's mouthpiece, a willing vessel that allows God to operate and use them to declare his thoughts and truths.

Be careful who you follow and what you believe. Unfortunately, in ministry there are many who boast on themselves and people follow along like stray puppies. They have a charming personality that draws people. Often leading them into situations and cults with individuals like Jim Jones or David Karesh. The danger is in getting your eye on man, worshipping him and looking to him instead of God.

Sheep get fleeced following a pastor or evangelist who boasts of great things. Yet, they always need more money and you have never seen any of the things they boast of. Don't believe someone is a prophet because they boast of it. Believe based on the fruit of what you hear and see. A true prophet speaks, and it happens. It doesn't always happen overnight, but it will happen just like it was spoken.

We ran across a gentleman who claimed to be a preacher. He could quote entire books of the bible in minutes. There was no anointing, he wasn't a vessel being used by God, he was a hireling. People heard his great feat and were charmed. They gave him great sums of money; but their souls were not edified. There was no healing, no deliverance and no offer of salvation. He came into town during revival and turned heads away from the preaching of the gospel. People saw something spectacular and thought it was supernatural.

Shakespearean actors recite long and arduous soliloquies. People with photographic memories read something one time and repeat it word for word. Always let the proof be in the pudding. The bible says to taste and see the Lord is good. Don't let the wolf trick you by wearing a fancy sheep skin jacket.

QUESTIONS

1. Have you ever heard a true prophet? If not, stop and search for Kim Clement on YouTube. Kim passed away in 2016, but the things he prophesied are still coming true; even about President Trump. What did you feel as you listened? Do you think God still has prophets in the land?

2. Where there is a real, there's always a fake. Real Coke or generic, Coach purses or knockoffs; differences may be subtle, but they are there. Have you ever experienced the fake? In church or out. A tribute band? An Elvis impersonator? What was your experience?

3. I'm amazed by illusionists and sleight of hand artists. I never know how they do it! Scam artists are illusionists. Promising you one thing while stealing from you in the same breath. People can be nice to your face while sticking a knife in your back? Did you see it coming or were you totally caught off

guard? Have you ever had an experience where the truth was nothing like what you saw in front of your eyes? What happened?

4. All Simon wanted was to be the center of attention. To be recognized and marveled at. He wasn't concerned about the people. How do remain humble; even when you are in the spotlight?

5. Cults are illusions. They talk about being a family; while cutting you off from yours. They create a private world, where you become totally dependent on them, as they take everything from you. How do we avoid cults? How do we see past the illusion?

STOP THE BLEEDING

Psalm 147:3
"He health the broken in heart, and bindeth up their wounds."

The Psalmist sings the greatness of God in this psalm. He extols his kindness and his abilities.

THINK ON THIS...
So many wounds, so many gashes within our hearts, our souls and our minds but God is faithful to stitch each one closed. To bind them up tight and to stop the bleeding.

God stops the bleeding. He is the healing balm that soothes and comforts. He is the one who draws out every pain. When the pain stops, it can then become a memory. At that point we have overcome. At that point, we have a testimony. Only with a testimony can you grow and love on somebody else.

When I was wounded and bleeding, I was consumed by my misery. I could feign a smile, I could hug someone and pray; but let's be honest, when you are hurting you can never give 100% of yourself to someone else. When you are wounded and bleeding you will never have the fullness of joy God desires for you. You will never be whole or well.

Jesus willingly paid for your healing, whether it is physical, emotional or spiritual. Everyone can quote a portion of Isaiah 53:5 but do you know the entire verse? It says, *"But he was wounded for our transgressions, he was bruised for our iniquities: the chastisement of our peace was upon him; and with his stripes we are healed."*

By his stripes we ARE healed. He was mocked and scorned so we could have peace. He was wounded, he was bruised, he stood in for us. He knows how it feels to be beaten, lied on, bullied if you will. He knows how it feels and he doesn't want you to hurt like that.

I find some people seem to like their wounds. They complain relentlessly of how people use them. Of how people walk all over them and hurt them over and over again in a million different ways. Yet, they stay in that same place. Even when you offer assistance, they reject it. They prefer sympathy over wholeness. Did you ever watch Winnie The Pooh? They have Eeyore mentalities. He was dismal, depressed, pessimistic and every other negative characteristic you can think of. He was slow and gloomy. No matter how happy or excited you were he could bring you down in a second.

That is not the life God has intended for any of us. God would rather we were more like Pooh. Pooh had his eyes set on honey and by golly he was going to get to it no matter what it took. We need to have our eyes on Jesus like that. We need to take every wound, every care, every hurt to Jesus and allow him to kiss it, to stitch it, to heal it. I'm ok with a scar. Scars remind us of where we came from, stupid things we did, times when it could have been a lot worse. Every scar on your body is a testimony to how you have lived, what you have been through. So are the emotional scars, the spiritual scars, the scars others can't see. Some scars seem to appear only when it is important for us to share that hurt, that time in our life for the benefit of someone else. Those are the scars that carry too much memory and can way us down. Other scars are a constant reminder that we are stronger now. Some would argue Jesus takes all the scars away.   I believe he leaves us with some; so we don't forget where we came from and they leave us with no desire to go back.

QUESTIONS

1. Are you still bleeding? What hurts haven't you fully turned over to God? Why are you still holding on to them?

2. What is your thought on emotional and spiritual scars? Do you think you have them? Or do you think He removes them? There are no right or wrong answers. Just your own personal opinion.

3. Do you feel your testimony could stop other people from bleeding? Could you be the first responder or EMT, spiritually speaking, who addresses the injury and gets them to the altar to be stitched up? What is there about your testimony that can reach another person?

4. Sometimes, those who are supposed to help us, cause more issues. Like hospitals, you go in for one thing and pick up something else. The same is true for churches. People are just people, even when they are Christians. Sometimes we hurt one another. People think they are being helpful; but instead cause great pain. Do you have any experience in this area? What is it?

5. How do we bind those wounds? How do we prevent them from infecting us to the point where we drop out of church and fall away from Jesus?

TAKING THE GOOD WITH THE BAD

2 KINGS 5:27
*"The leprosy therefore of Naaman shall cleave unto thee,
and unto thy seed forever. And he went out from his
a leper as white as snow."*

Elisha's servant, Gehazi, got greedy. Naaman was an
honorable man who had favor with his master. He came to
Elisha looking to be healed of Leprosy. Once he was clean
and whole, he offered Elisha many things; all of which Elisha
turned down. Elisha wasn't taking credit nor was he taking
any of the glory for what God had done. Gehazi however,
went behind Elisha's back. He followed after Namaan, lied
to him and was given garments and silver. Then he lied to
Elisha about where he had been.

THINK ON THIS...
Did you know spirits can attach themselves to inanimate
objects? Like items you purchase at a yard sale or off of
Craigslist. I know it might sound strange, but it is true none
the less.

Randy and I had donated some items to a gentleman from
our church. He had an orphanage in Haiti and he would ship
clothing and household items down to sell; thereby raising
money to take care of the children. To thank us he had a
wooden mug made with our names on it. (The names were
misspelled but the cup was intended for us.) We
appreciated it and I placed it on a shelf in our living room.
It wasn't long after that Randy got sick. I mean flat on his
back sick. It felt like kidney stones and it made him feel bad
all over. This went on for over a month! We visited the ER
twice during this time. Neither time were there any stones
actually blocking or in the ducts. There were stones being
formed, a few the first time and more the second, but were
clearly not the reason for the disabling pain he was
experiencing. Randy ran a tree service, a physical and
demanding job but had no strength or ability. We had to

rely on his dad and brother to cover his jobs so everything coming in financially was going back out to pay them for working and taking care of the business.

About 5 weeks in we went to a mid-week service and during the bible study that night we were reminded of how spirits can attach themselves to objects. I leaned over to Randy and whispered to him, "It's that cup we got from Haiti." It was like a lightbulb went on in my head. That night we went home, Randy took that cup out to the grill. He doused it with lighter fluid; not once but THREE times before it would burn. After that night there was no more pain, no more issues, no sickness. He got up and went to work.

In the same manner Gehazi was affected. He took the gift and received the spirit of infirmity that was attached to it. Talk about a hard lesson to learn. We have talked before about making a choice in our lives that affects more than just us. His moment of greed affected him and EVERY generation that came after him. Randy and I received a gift and therefore the curse could be lifted. Not so for Gehazi.

When we receive something under false pretenses, God sees that. When we lie to get gain, God sees that. God will bless you if you are faithful. He will meet the needs of those paying their tithes; the word says so in Malachi 3:10-11. Gehazi lied. He went behind Elisha's back; so the lesson Elisha was trying to teach Naaman about God was voided by Gehazi's selfish motives. When we become selfish, stepping into places where we are not meant to be, we cause a ripple that can negate and steal a blessing God was preparing. Gehazi caused a ripple that could have negatively affected Naaman in his new walk with God and he brought leprosy upon every generation of his family. The gain one receives through deceit is never worth the consequence that is meted out.

If God is blessing, don't think the enemy isn't laying snares and curses to trip you up. Today would be a good day to just put a little oil on your fingertips. Go about your house praying to break every strong hold, every curse, to bind every spirit that is not meant for your good. Run your fingertips over walls, objects, doorways, beds, pillows, knobs, computer keys, etc. Then notice as attitudes and behaviors change. You might be quite surprised at the differences in your home.

QUESTIONS

1. Did you learn in school that every action has an equal and opposite reaction? What does that mean?

2. Bugs Bunny would say, "If I do it, I get a whipping...I do it!" Gehazi knew Elisha was a true prophet of God. He knew God hid nothing from Elisha, knew he was taking a great risk by going to Naaman; yet he went and took everything he could get. Why would he do that? Why would he risk everything?

3. Have you ever done something knowing full well there would be a consequence for it? Why did you do it? Was it worth it in the end?

4. God gave all of us a freewill. He gave us the gift of choosing our actions and responses. Gehazi used his freewill to follow Naaman? Paul said everything was permissible for him but not everything was in his best interests. (I paraphrased there) People often want to know why God would allow certain things to happen. For example, mass shootings, rape, kidnapping, etc. Freewill can be used for good or for evil. It is the choice each of us makes with every thought that flows through our head. With that being said, can you now answer the question of why or how God can allow bad things to happen? Is it God's fault they happened?

5. Our actions might yield us something good, like the items Gehazi received of Naaman. However, the equal and opposite reaction might take a greater toll on us than we imagined. Do you think Gehazi ever imagined he would receive leprosy for his choice? Ultimately, who is responsible for the choices you make? Do you have any excuse when you know it is wrong to begin with? Why do we make excuses then?

VENGEANCE

DEUTERONOMY 32:35

"To me belongeth vengeance, and recompense' their foot shall slide in due time: for the day of their calamity is at hand, and the things that shall come upon them make haste."

This verse is part of the song of Moses. Moses knew who his God was and what his promises were. He had walked with God, talked with God and had seen with his own eyes how God could recompense the enemy on his behalf.

THINK ON THIS...

When someone does you wrong, do you get upset when thunderbolts don't immediately rip through the atmosphere to strike them down there and then? We don't often see swift judgement. It seems like the worse a person behaves the more respect they receive or the greater their gain. We see it with the Hollywood crowd all the time. We see it with politicians who are crooked and evil. We even see it at our own personal level with people we work with or have been associated with for one reason or another. How come they prosper and there doesn't seem to be any consequences for their actions?!

I have a one-word answer for you...Grace. They receive the same gift of grace you and I have received. If it weren't for grace, which one of us would be left standing? Grace creates a space of time for us to realize the depth of our sin and the consequences it brings with it. If it were not for grace which of us would have ever made it to the altar to repent and be forgiven? Most of us would have been struck down a hundred times over had judgement been swift and immediate.

Grace doesn't necessarily preclude you from receiving consequences in this life. Jails are full of people who have received punishment for their crimes. There are murderers on death row in every state prison across America. Yet vengeance still belongs to the Lord. There is still an eternal reward or an eternal punishment for those same crimes and for the crimes, hurts, pain, distress, etc that go unnoticed; unless it has been covered under the blood.

Whatever has happened in your life. Whoever has hurt you, physically, mentally or emotionally God knows. Next to the name of that person it is written down and God is keeping an account. For now, grace is covering that person. Pray for them. I know it is hard. Those prayers will either see that person saved and changed or it will rain down heaping coals of fire and judgement upon them.

Grace is holding up judgement. Don't be upset by it, because again, that same grace held up judgment on you; so you could get it right and have the hope of eternal life in the presence of Jesus.

QUESTIONS

1. Is there someone you have failed to forgive because of the hurt they inflicted on you? What did they do? How long ago did it happen?

2. Do you know what the bible says about forgiveness? How many times are we supposed to forgive someone? If we fail to forgive, can we be forgiven?

3. Is there anyone in your past whom you've hurt? Perhaps they are still waiting for you to receive your just desserts. Have you ever asked them to forgive you? You should. Before you take communion again you should ask for forgiveness and forgive those who hurt you. Make a list here of those you need to speak to. You can do it by phone, email, text message, however you can reach out to them.

4. In the Old Testament failure to repent and change could end by being stoned! How does it make you feel, to know grace allowed you to come to an understanding and knowledge of Jesus Christ? God gave you a grace period. Let that sink in. You could have been a pile of rubble.

5. Matthew 43:44 says, "But I say unto you, love your enemies, bless them that curse you, do good to them that hate you, and pray for them who despitefully use you, and persecute you;" That is one tall order, but can you do it? Understanding that grace is at work in all of our lives, that we all receive a grace period, can you pray for those who come against you?

WITNESSES

HEBREWS 12:1

*"Wherefore seeing we also are compassed about with
so great a cloud of witnesses, let us lay aside every
weight, and the sin which doth so easily beset us, and
let us run with patience the race that is set before us,"*

In the previous chapter of Hebrews, Paul has just recounted
men and women of God who have accomplished great
things through their faith. They knew God's voice, they
believed God, they trusted God, they did what was asked
regardless of how strange it sounded and now each of them
is remembered by all of us.

THINK ON THIS...

I have read this verse, heard this verse and never really
comprehended exactly what it meant until today. I love how
God speaks a word, shows me something new, or lets me
read a phrase and suddenly the scripture just opens up
before me and the little light bulb goes on above my head.

Paul is saying all those folks from Chapter 11 are witnesses
to us. Their lives are a testimony to us. Proving you can
live this life, working out your own soul salvation and
growing in God. You can look at their lives and see how God
moved on their behalf. You can see how God asked them to
do what seemed impossible, like building an ark and filling it
with animals, and gave them the ability, instruction and
wisdom to complete the task set before them. You can trust
God when he asks you to sacrifice and give your most
precious possession. Like Abraham trusted God when he
told him to sacrifice Isaac. He knew Isaac was his promise.
He knew Isaac was the avenue to all the nations he would
be the father of. Abraham knew God promised him and
could not lie. We need to understand God will create a path
for us to walk; where we prosper and not lose.

The witnesses are there to remind us if we slip, if we should fall into a temptation, repentance is available. Forgiveness will always be extended. We have this great gift called grace. Don't abuse it. It's not there so we can sin but IF we should sin. God has promised if we our tempted he will create a way of escape. You just need to call on him. *"No temptation has overtaken you except what is common to mankind. And God is faithful; he will not let you be tempted beyond what you can bear. But when you are tempted, he will also provide a way out so that you can endure it."* 1 Corinthians 10:13 (NIV)

God is so faithful to us. He created us to fellowship with him. God wants to visit with us. Adam and Eve messed it all up though. They gave away the dominion of the earth. God created the law then, so people knew what was right and what was wrong. Ultimately, he gave us his only begotten son. Jesus took our place. His blood was the price of our soul. Jesus gave his life to ransom our lives back. He shed his blood to cleanse all our iniquities. He promised to carry our burdens, to create a place for us in heaven, and when we finish our race there will be a reward waiting for us.

One day Jesus is coming back! We will reign with him. One day we will get to meet Jesus and our great cloud of witnesses! Imagine hearing David, Moses, Noah, Peter, Paul and Jesus tell us their life stories. We won't just read about them anymore. We will sit down, sup together, laugh together and rejoice at the trials we endured here which allowed us to be together there. Oh, happy day.

QUESTIONS

1. When you read about this the cloud of witnesses, do you realize they went through the same struggles we do? We may live in a different century, a different dispensation of time and yet our struggles aren't any different. Can you think of a struggle you have been through that matches up with someone in Hebrews 11?

2. While we have a cloud of witnesses in Hebrews 11, do you have people in your circle of influence who you consider to be witnesses? People who have been through some trials and trusted God? People whose testimonies encourage you and give you hope? Who are they?

3. Would you consider yourself a witness? If your name was included in Hebrews 11 what would it say about you?

4. Hebrews 11 gives us a list of some awesome people and it says there are many more. Who in the bible do you find to be a witness to you? Write down what you would say about them.

5. Everyday people, like you and me, became known as the heroes of faith. Like us, they had to step by faith when God called them. I know people, who know they are called, yet they have failed to step out. Why don't we step when we know, that we know, God has called us?

DON'T BE AN ACCESSORY

ACTS 8:18-19

"And when Simon saw that through laying on of the apostles' hands the Holy Ghost was given, he offered them money, Saying, Give me also this power, that on whomsoever I lay hands, he may receive the Holy Ghost."

Simon the sorcerer wanted the Holy Ghost as an accessory. He saw the Holy Ghost as one more reason for people to seek him out and desire what he could provide. He didn't want the relationship with God, he didn't want the Holy Ghost for himself. He only wanted to pay for the ability to impart the Holy Ghost to someone else. As if the Holy Ghost were a cheap magician's trick in a circus side show.

THINK ON THIS...

Simon was looking for the Holy Ghost to be an accessory for him. Something he would give to others at a cost. Something that made him look good, gave him prestige, one more item in his bag of tricks if you will. Have you ever met people who were all about their accessories?

I don't want to be an accessory of Jesus; nor do I want him to be my accessory. An accessory on its own is useless. An accessory is like window dressing. You can pay a LOT of money for window dressings and still be missing all of the greatest treasures in life. Accessories don't add a cent to your personal value or worth. They don't keep you company, care for you when you are ill or hurt, share in your emotions or invest anything back into you.

You can put a string of pearls around a pig's neck but guess what? It's still a pig. Accessories don't change who you are, they can't alter your past or pave a way for your future. Sometimes we use accessories as a way to create a new persona for our self, but they only create an illusion of who we want to be.

Men drape mistresses in jewelry and furs but she will never have his last name. She will never inherit what he has, she will never be seen by his friends or be an intimate part of what or who truly matters in his life. In truth, she is only an accessory herself. Something to buy that he will eventually toss away or pass along.

People pray and call on the name of Jesus only in times of trouble. When they present themselves as godly only on Sunday, when they call themselves Christians but all of their attributes are worldly; they have made Jesus an accessory in their life. They have committed the same trespass as Simon the Sorcerer. Wanting Him but denying the power of Him. Denying His authority, position, and ability.

Where does Jesus fit into your life? Is he an accessory you hide in your bag of tricks? Do you drape him around you in a flashy show? Or is he your friend and companion in all that you do?

As for me, He is my friend, my king, my savior and the list goes on. He is the one I talk to when no one else is around. The one I confide in, the one I tell my deepest hurts to, He knows my strongest desires and everything in between. I love him and he loves me.

Don't allow yourself to be an accessory either. Used when people need something but not good enough to just hang out with. The date when no one else is available. Don't be used and abused by anyone because you are worth much more than that. Don't let anyone EVER tell you otherwise. Don't be an accessory.

QUESTIONS

1. What is your definition of an accessory?

2. Has anyone ever treated you like an accessory? They only call when they need something? Only call when they want to tell you their big news? How does it make you feel?

3. How do you handle it when someone treats you like an accessory? Do you go along with it just happy to be included? Then crumble when they reject you the next time? Is there a better way to handle the situation?

4. Have you ever treated Jesus like he was your accessory? Did you realize that was what you were doing? Are you still doing it? Do you only have him around when it's convenient for you?

5. Do you share everything with Jesus? Good, bad, joyful, victorious, uncertain? Is he your friend & companion?

THE PRICE OF BEING A LEADER

DEUTERONOMY 34:4-5, 7

"And the Lord said unto him, This is the land which I sware unto Abraham, unto Isaac, and unto Jacob, saying, I will give it unto thy seed: I have caused thee to see it with thine eyes, but thou shalt not go over thither. So Moses the servant of the Lord died there in the land of Moab, according to the word of the Lord... And Moses was an hundred and twenty years old when he died."

Moses had led the people out of Israel, wandered through the desert 40 years and now, at 120 years old, stands on Mt. Pisgah; where he is able to survey the promised land. His eyes can feast upon the lush and fertile grounds where rest will eventually be found for the people. Land he will never live in, never step upon, never taste or experience. He has reached the end of his journey.

THINK ON THIS...

Being the leader doesn't always mean you get the prize. Moses has endured these people for 40 years. He has listened to their whining, stood in the gap when they offended God, prayed for direction to move forward when everyone else wanted to quit and return. I think Moses found out what it's like to be a mom. Someone is always yelling, "Mommy, mommy, mommy!" Because they are hurt, mad, rejected, dirty, hungry, thirsty and on and on. Someone is always looking to you to fix what is wrong.

It is only in growing and maturing that children learn mom can't fix every hurt. She can't fix a broken heart or a broken promise. She can't take the test for you and she isn't always within ear shot when you need to make an important decision or to stand for what you know is right.

The same holds true for Moses and the children of Israel. You can only take them so far. You instill right things into them, so they learn to treat others fairly. You teach them to share, to pray, to be respectful, to love others the way you yourself want to be loved.

I was thinking about the Olympics and all the coaches behind those great athletes. They put in the time, the work, they put in a lot of sweat and hours but when the gold medals are given out there are no coaches standing on the podium. They recognition is different. They are paid for their services. Their work is known among their peers. Their reputation has up and coming athletes searching them out. They may not have a gold medal to wear around their neck but there is great reward in seeing your protégés accomplishments.

Moses never entered the promise land but he was still rewarded. No one knows where he is buried because God took care of that himself. He is recorded in the Hebrews Hall of Faith. He was seen on the Mt of Transfiguration with Jesus. Moses was a true friend of God. Can you imagine being able to be so entrenched in the Spirit of God you come away glowing? Or spending 40 days and nights twice in the presence of God or having a burning bush talk to you?

Lead on, if that is what you are called to do. If someone else gets the medal, the recognition, the reward, don't concern yourself over it. God's reward program is so much greater than any honor man will ever bestow. To know I pleased God, that he smiles when he looks down on me, to think he might go that's my Amy, brings tears to my eyes.

QUESTIONS

1. Have you ever worked hard and been recognized for it? Maybe you won an award, received a certificate, diploma, etc. Why were you recognized and what did you receive?

2. Did you ever work hard and someone else received the prize or the recognition? Maybe you worked behind the scenes or in conjunction with someone. Like Moses you led the way, so to speak, but didn't get to the promise land.

3. Have you ever been in the leader? We tend to think the leader has it made. The truth is, the leader has more headaches, less sleep and generally less fun. Who were you leading and what was your experience?

4. When I worked at Disney, we would have large groups of Cubans come into the park. The leader carried a flag and everyone had on matching T-shirts. Where the flag went, the group went. As a character, you learned to take the flag. It was the only way to move and safely extricate yourself from the throng of the crowd. As the leader all eyes are on you. Your every move is being watched. One wrong step and not only will you fall over the cliff but everyone watching goes too. As a Christian, is your walk strong enough to lead? Be honest, if people are watching you, is your walk going to cause them to stumble or will it raise the standard they live by?

5. Being a leader can also come with huge sacrifices. Think about your pastor. Do you know where he makes sacrifices in order to be a good shepherd to the church?

SCRIPTURE BLIND

JOHN 5:39
"Search the scriptures; for in them ye think ye have eternal life: and they are they which testify of me.."

Jesus has just healed the man laying by the pool of Bethesda, on the Sabbath day no less. You would think people would be rejoicing but instead the Jews were beside themselves at his audacity. Imagine healing someone on the Sabbath. You were not supposed to do any kind of work, even a good work. It is, after all, the day of rest. They were stuck on a couple of scriptures instead of the whole word of God. Stuck on the letter that kills, instead of on the Spirit which gives life.

THINK ON THIS...
Jewish men spent a lot of time in the synagogue reasoning together the meaning of scriptures. Always looking for the deeper, hidden messages God had left them. I was thinking about this the other day, if these men studied the word day in and day, out how come they were looking for a full-blown regal king; instead of a baby?

When Jesus was born, only four men were anticipating and watching for him. The three Wisemen and Simeon (Luke 2:25-30). How is it that all those other men, sitting and reasoning together had not understood that the Messiah would come as a baby? Isaiah 9:6 says, "Unto us a child is born, unto us a son is given." Seems plain and clear doesn't it?

The Wisemen knew to watch for the star and they had their gifts ready to go. They were willing to travel approximately two years just to give their offering and see the baby, to see the King of kings, the Lord of lords. I wonder if they had tried to tell anybody else. If so, I bet people laughed at them and mocked them. What do you think?

See they all had the same scriptures, same old testament we have today, but not everyone chose to believe the whole of the scripture. They got hung up on the King status, hung up on the part of coming to deliver God's people, hung up on the scriptures they picked out. They became scripture blind if you will. Blind to what they didn't understand or want to believe.

I pray that you are not scripture blind. It is a rampant issue in society today. People want to pick and choose the scriptures they adhere too. They basically throw the baby out with the bath water. Are you familiar with that saying? It comes from when families filled a big tub and everyone from Dad on down used the same water to bathe. By the time the baby used the water it was rather dirty and dark and who could see what was in it. If you aren't careful you can throw out something very important and priceless.

I hope you will be cautious in your handling and understanding of scripture and you will think twice when someone tells you that certain scriptures don't apply anymore or that certain scriptures were only for then and that span of time.

All scripture is God breathed and important for all men. Every scripture in the Old Testament points to the events of the New Testament and even to what's happening in our world today! There are times and events in the Old Testament that tell about days still to come. Every word ever written in scripture was meant for us. It guides, instructs, heals, and so much more. It truly is an instruction book for our lives.

QUESTIONS

1. Are there any scriptures in the bible, which you feel, are not relevant to your life today? Or to society or the church as a whole? Write the chapter and verse(s) down here.

2. If you chose more than one verse, take just one and explain why you feel it isn't relevant.

3. Are you watching for Jesus to return? Do you know how and where he is returning? You can find it if you search the scriptures? Write your thoughts here of how he is coming and where.

4. Do you see anything happening in the world that points to being in the "End Times" as scripture describes them? What do you see? Why do you think it is a sign?

5. Do you believe in a "catching away" (rapture)? Why or why not? Can you back it up with scripture? If so what scripture?

SUPPORTERS

1 CHRONICLES 11:18
"And the three brake through the host of the Philistines, and drew water by the gate, and took it, and brought it to David: but David would not drink of it, but poured it out to the LORD,"

David and his men were surrounded by the Philistines, when David spoke aloud his need for a drink of water. Three of his mightiest men took it upon themselves to provide that drink at the risk and peril of their own lives.

THINK ON THIS...
In my flesh, my first thought was, "And he poured it out!" Three men risked their lives to get him a drink and he poured it on the ground. Then I realized, he gave that life-giving water to the Lord as an offering. What would we have done in David's shoes?

Have you ever received a gift from somebody and passed it on to somebody else? Perhaps they had a greater need for it? Randy and I have been in services where someone came up for prayer and their need for a financial blessing was great. It was so great we gave them an offering out of our pocket. We have even given the offering that was taken up for us to the person or persons standing in front of him. Not because we are anything great or wonderful but because the Lord put the burden upon us and we answered.

David's need for a drink of water was great but the need for the safety and well-being of his men was even greater. David took their sacrifice and sacrificed it to the Lord in thanksgiving for the love and support of those courageous men.

See David had always fought side by side with his men. He never asked them to do anything he wasn't willing to do himself. He cared about them and he saw to their needs and he gave to them out of every spoil that was accrued. When you go the extra mile for others, others go the extra mile for you. I believe each one of those men knew if they had been the one in desperate need of a drink or food that David would have risked his life for them.

In ministry it is a tremendous blessing to be surrounded by people who look out for you. God has blessed us with people who feed us, shelter us, give us a place to park and plug the bus in, who give because they find great value in what we do for Jesus. They also do it because they feel the burden from God to give.

How awesome is my God who knows my every need and supplies them? He not only supplies the needs but the wants as well. I make my request known and he pulls it off every time. I need to brag on the love of my Jesus for me. It is greater than anything else I know.

I wonder, what kind of people are surrounding you? Do you have people around you who give or just take? Find people who have the same heart you have. Not because we expect something back when we are kind but because it is so wonderful to be appreciated and cared for in due season.

QUESTIONS

1. Do you have friends who appreciate you or use you? What kind of friend are you?

2. Have you ever wanted something, received it, and then given it away because someone else needed it more than you? What was it and how did you feel about giving it away?

3. Has anybody ever gone out of their way for you? Did you need groceries, have a bill you were desperate to pay, needed help after surgery or an accident? What did they do for you?

4. If you were David would you have poured out the water? Or would you have drank it? Be honest. How would you have felt about someone risking their life to bring you that drink?

5. When is the last time you gave an offering, to God in thanks, for the people he has placed around you? Rather it was a financial offering or a praise offering, did you remember God?

ON THE EVE

Ezra 3:12-13

"But many of the priests and Levites and chief of the fathers, who were ancient men, that had seen the first house, when the foundation of this house was laid before their eyes, wept with a loud voice; and many shouted aloud for joy: So that the people could not discern the noise of the shout of joy from the noise of the weeping of the people: for the people shouted with a loud shout, and the noise was heard afar off."

The people were rebuilding the temple. The one Solomon built was of great splendor he had everything overlaid in gold; everything was large and ornate. Beautiful would scarcely describe it but it had been destroyed. Everything had been taken by the enemy and only rubble was left behind.

THINK ON THIS:

The people made a sound that was noise abroad. From a distance no one could tell it was a sound of mixed feelings. They didn't know some were excited and still others were grieved in their hearts.

Amongst the crowd that day were men who had seen the splendor of the first temple. They remembered its opulence and grandeur. It was fit for a king, for The King. Now, here stands the beginnings of a very humble structure. All the gold is gone, the sea is gone, the beautiful pillars were gone, everything that once was had since been carried away. They cried that day. A great lament of what they had, of the memories they shared arose from their lips.

Mingled within that same crowd were people who had never set foot in the original temple. They had never partaken of the things of God. Now, they were observing the feasts, sacrificing as God had prescribed for their sins. They were learning to walk in his ways and precepts. They were excited to see the foundation laid. It represented a new beginning. They felt the same excitement we feel when we first give our life to Christ. Everything was new and they wanted to shout it for everyone to hear.

People today are just like these two groups. As we face a New Year some are excited at the prospect of a new beginning. There is something about the clock striking midnight and everything is supposed to be different from the last 12 months. It is like an invisible barrier. It blocks all the bad and old from the new and possible.

Then you have those who are always looking backwards. They continually live in the past. They reminisce and those old memories become more fantastic than the truth of the matter. The real problem is that nothing that happens in their present and future can ever compare to their memory. Have you ever had that happen to you? My grandma would make lemon pudding for me when I was a kid. She cooked it on the stove and when it cooled down, she would beat the egg whites into a meringue and fold them in. It was the best tasting stuff you ever had. Just writing about it I can almost taste it. My grandma died over 30 years ago. Since then I have only made lemon pudding a couple of times and every time, I am disappointed. It never lives up to my memory of it.

There is nothing wrong with a great memory, so long as we realize we can't live in it forever. I like to think about the time I spent with my grandma. We watched Rockford Files together and she would pop popcorn in bacon grease for us. Sometimes she would bake cookies and I would eat them up while they were fresh and hot. She always cooked special meals for us to share and we would sleep in her big bed at night. When it was cold, she would fill the hot water bottle and put it down by our feet and we would always talk until I fell asleep. I loved her and she loved me, her death left a huge void in my life.

I couldn't live in my memories of her forever though. I had to continue on with my life. I had to grow up and have a daughter of my own and live in the present so I could embrace all the moments God had for me.

As you journey through life let go of all the things that hold you back. All the things that cause you to not value what is before you. Look forward. Remember yesterday with fondness but be content with today.

QUESTIONS

1. Have you ever had to start over? Maybe your house caught fire, you went through a hurricane, tornado or earthquake. Maybe you had to move. How did you feel about the new place?

2. I know someone whose son died. He was a grown man. He was a good man; but when he was alive the family would fuss at him for missing family dinners and such because of other commitments. Today their memories make him sound like a superhero. Like he had never disappointed them. Do you know anyone like that? Or maybe you have a memory like that. Who is it and what were they really like?

3. Do you have a memory like the addict? A memory that tends to pull you back to a time and place that is better left alone? The addict's memories will soon have them jonesing for another fix. Memories can lead us backwards, back into sin and rebellion. What memory pulls you backwards? Write down the place, person or event and then re-write it so it accurately reflects the truth. Writing the truth will help you from stepping back into it.

4. Why do certain moments, circumstances or events look so much better in hindsight?

5. As we are on the brink of a New Year and this is the last question of the year have you changed? Thinking back on each of the devotions which one truly impacted you? What are you taking away that has strengthened your walk and made you closer to Christ?

Made in the USA
Lexington, KY
06 November 2019